A RADICAL SUFFRAGIST

in

WASHINGTON, D.C.

AN INSIDE STORY OF THE NATIONAL WOMAN'S PARTY

SHIRLEY M. MARSHALL

THE
History
PRESS

Published by The History Press
Charleston, SC
www.historypress.com

All cover photos courtesy of the Library of Congress. *Front cover, top*: Map with White House and Lafayette Square, 1919. *Baist's Real Estate Surveys of Washington, D.C. Inset*: Elizabeth Kalb holding a banner, 1918. *Bottom*: Elizabeth Kalb in a demonstration, 1918. *Back cover, top*: "Woman Suffrage, Arrests." *Harris & Ewing, 1917. Inset:* Sheet music, "Votes for Women International Suffrage Song." *Ed. Markel, 1916.*

First published 2024

Manufactured in the United States

ISBN 9781467155885

Library of Congress Control Number: 2023947091

If it takes a village to raise a child, this book took a city.
Heartfelt thanks to family, friends, librarians and historians.
And especially to Elizabeth, who started it all.

CONTENTS

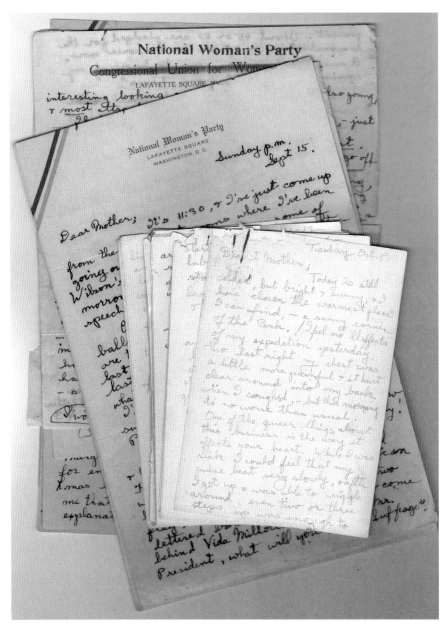

Letters from Elizabeth Kalb to her mother, Benigna Kalb, during her time as a suffragist, 1918–1919. *Handy/Marshall Collection.*

PREFACE

Elizabeth Kalb Green Handy entered my life in childhood when we visited her farm home in Virginia. Mostly my memories are of sunny days exploring their woods, being scared to death by the cow and eating fresh-baked scones. A kindly, small, white-haired lady, Elizabeth passed away while I was in high school.

Yet her story was so compelling. She had been a suffragist! Been sick in jail and had to be removed so she wouldn't become a "martyr"! There was more to her story, but that part especially stayed with me.

Years later, my father inherited the papers of Elizabeth and her husband. Imagine my delight on discovering her letters, giving blow-by-blow accounts of life in Washington in 1918. The letters opened up a new Elizabeth: an adventurous, observant young woman having a grand time fighting for women's rights.

Elizabeth's mother, Benigna, had kept the letters through many years and moves. When she passed, Elizabeth boxed them up with other papers and stored them at her farm in Virginia. The letters survived mice, decluttering and a flooded basement. Finally, my mother and sister rescued them from the farm.

Reading her other papers, I was stunned at the diversity of Elizabeth's life experience. She helped with Native American water rights in California, for instance, and reported on China's civil war.

But we start where Elizabeth's adventures began—in Washington, D.C. She arrived as a volunteer with the National Woman's Party, fighting for the right to vote.

Chapter 1

WHAT ARE WE FIGHTING FOR?

The right of citizens of the United States to vote shall not be denied or abridged by the United States or by any State on account of sex. Congress shall have power to enforce this article by appropriate legislation.
—Nineteenth Amendment, first presented in Congress
by Senator Sargent (R-CA), 1878

When Elizabeth Kalb[1] arrived in Washington in 1918, a world war and the battle for women's suffrage both appeared headed to victory.

American troops had been fighting for over a year in Europe. These fresh soldiers and munitions made a crucial difference to the Allies' four years of hard slog and slaughter. As they pushed on into Germany, rumors spread of a possible end to the war.

For suffragists, meanwhile, the long struggle had at last gained traction. Beginning in the West, women had started winning state voting rights. These new female voters provided fresh support to organizations fighting for national suffrage.

The suffrage amendment was first submitted to Congress in 1878, finally voted on in 1887—and defeated. The next vote did not come until 1914. Again, it failed, but hope was revived. Now, in September 1918, the House had already passed the amendment and the Senate was set to vote soon.

The revival of suffrage was part of a rapidly changing American society.

This music was written after New York women won state suffrage. Women getting more independent each day! Jack Stern and William Tracy, 1918. *Library of Congress.*

ORGANIZED WOMEN: Women's clubs grew exponentially in the late 1800s, bringing strength of unity and greater public presence. Both Black and White women, apart and together, used these groups to actively promote social causes.

EDUCATION, TECHNOLOGY AND EMPLOYMENT GROWTH: More women had opportunities for college and careers beginning in the late 1800s. For instance, the number of doctors, as well as office workers, was increasing. The war also meant new jobs for unskilled workers, especially women, with increased demand in manufacturing and agriculture.

NEW POLITICS: Many working-class European immigrants brought with them a desire to promote social justice and equal rights. Through unions, clubs and new political parties, both men and women were engaging more in these struggles.

RACIAL AND OTHER CHANGES: Southern Black Americans, oppressed by Jim Crow laws, were beginning to move north—although they were often met with resentment and violence there, too. Combined with increased immigration, this movement led to more urbanization of the country.

And with war raging in Europe, educated middle- and upper-class women were leading efforts to support soldiers and refugees, raise funds and plan for peace. These more prominent public roles gained women's suffrage additional political support.

President Wilson had been lukewarm at best in support of voting rights for women. But in January 1918, he asked Congress to pass the suffrage amendment. Passed by the House, only the Senate vote remained. If they approved it, the amendment could go to the states for ratification. If the Senate voted down the amendment, however, the entire process must start over with the next Congress.

A constitutional amendment requires Congress to pass the proposal with at least two-thirds of both House and Senate approving. The proposal must then be ratified by two-thirds of the states for the amendment to become law. In 1918, that meant fifty-six senators must vote "yea" to move the proposal to the states.

The struggle to gain women this civil right appeared near an end, but the final count was still too close to call. Suffrage supporters were needed in Washington to thank current Senate supporters, to encourage those wavering and to push anti-suffrage members to change their minds.

PRO- AND ANTI-SUFFRAGISTS

Support for women's suffrage generally fell within two arguments: equality (women are equal to men and should have the same rights) and maternity (women are caretakers of children and society, so they need the power to improve their conditions).

Anti-suffragists did not directly deny women's equality or their central role as mothers, but they viewed their entry into politics as a dangerous move for society. Leaders, both men and women, had supporters across the states and a lobbying office in Washington, D.C. The following are the major arguments they used to keep women from the polls.

STATE'S RIGHTS AND RACE: Many antis claimed suffrage was an issue for each state to determine. That argument resonated particularly with southern White people resentful of existing federal mandates giving Black men the right to vote. Although Jim Crow laws had eviscerated most of that right, resentment remained.

And some people especially feared that southern Black women were more likely than men to vote. Senator John Williams (D-MS) wrote to suffragist Helen Hamilton Gardener, "[Black women] cannot be controlled, as the men can be, and they would almost all, without exception, go to the polls while a great many white women would not."[2] The violent intimidation used on Black men, he believed, could not be used against women in the same way.[3]

LOSS OF POWER: Both men and women were concerned that a change in status would hurt the existing social structure. These arguments included:

Women are the "moral center" of family and nation. Politics is a dirty but necessary arena. Women's participation would corrupt them, lessening all women's social capital.

Voting will break up marriages and homes. Mothers are responsible for their children's upbringing and social well-being, as well as for running the home. Children will lose attention and care—as will husbands—if women enter politics. (Ironically, suffrage supporters used the idea of "mother as caretaker" to argue that women needed the vote to protect children and community.)

Men are providers and protectors. Women's participation in politics will diminish men's ability to care for their families. And women might vote contrary to their husbands, despite wives' "ignorance" of government and business.

Kewpie dolls for suffrage: Mothers need to protect their children, and the United States' "No Taxation Without Representation" applies to women. Rose O'Neill. *Puck* magazine, 1915. *Library of Congress.*

ANTI-SUFFRAGE
No. 168

Socialists are Suffragists, Pacifists, and Feminists.

Pacifists are usually Suffragists. Socialists and Feminists.

Feminists are Suffragists, Socialists, and generally Pacifists.

Suffrage leaders in every country are Socialists, Feminists and generally Pacifists.

The four movements are in reality all one.

Socialism, Anarchy and Pro-German doctrines taught in the public schools of Denver.

Elihu Root does NOT favor Woman Suffrage.

Another Pankhurst jailed.

Everyone familiar with the personnel of suffrage leadership knows that if the socialist-pacifist-feminist element were eliminated there would be neither leaders nor a cause to lead.

Gov. Lowden, the state government, and the state council of defense. The convention, which was held in the West Side auditorium, from which the pacifists, led by the Socialists and some

aganda has never been a part education, former school board shown a disposition to give t wide latitude in this direction. now on. President Hallett ex the board will summarily dismi teacher who attempts to make | speeches, or distribute political ganda to the pupils.

The ultimatum of President caused a stir among the teach sembled for the purpose of org for the school term, which opens Others who spoke were Mrs. Grenfell, former state superinten schools, and Mrs. Emma Seldon, superintendent. Mrs. Mary C. C ford, state superintendent of pu struction, in addressing the t said: "Our slogan in the C schools should be 'Better than ev (Rocky Mt. News, Sept. 4.)

Denver schools once ranked Under the direction of these ladi have fallen inconceivably low.

A recent survey of the schools | ver discloses conditions almost belief. Ten per cent of the child tend basement school rooms, sau. almost like dungeons where the li seating and sanitary arrangemer atrocious. The survey states th CITY OF ITS SIZE IN THE (TRY IS DOING SO LITTLE THE HEALTH OF ITS SC

An example of anti-suffrage views by the Cambridge (Massachusetts) Anti-Suffrage Association, September 19, 1917. *Library of Congress.*

SOCIALISM/COMMUNISM: "The red follows the yellow" was one threat made by antis. In other words, socialism/communism follows suffrage. Then, as now, "socialism" was seen as threatening the American way of life and was a fearsome thing. Socialists were asking for not only equal rights in voting but also equal pay and an eight-hour workday.

WAR MEASURES POLICY: In 1917, Congress and President Wilson agreed to pass only legislative measures related to the war effort. Antis used this as a reason to sideline suffrage. But women played a major role in war work, from unskilled laborers to national leaders. While Wilson declared in 1918 that suffrage was a necessary "war measure," antis did not agree.

MODERATES AND RADICALS

Two very different groups led the final suffrage effort: the National American Woman Suffrage Association (NAWSA) and the National Woman's Party (NWP). Many other suffrage organizations existed, but these two were the most prominent and influential. They were also at opposite ends of the spectrum on campaign tactics.

NAWSA was large, well known and deeply entrenched politically. A national umbrella organization, with many diverse state priorities and constraints, NAWSA could not afford to get too far behind its members—or too far ahead. The members did not want another fifty years of the same hopes denied. Yet they also expected a certain level of respectability. Lobbying and parades were fine, but not "radical" or "militant" action.

For many years, NAWSA had focused on gaining individual state suffrage. While it maintained connections to federal politicians, few resources were allocated to that effort. But this began to change after 1915. As some state efforts faltered or failed, the limits of this strategy became clear. Under the leadership of Carrie Chapman Catt, in 1916, NAWSA refocused on a federal campaign while still maintaining state efforts.

NAWSA's main effort in Washington was "soft" lobbying. This meant staying in constant, friendly touch with politicians and state leaders. The women did not confront but cajoled, befriended and educated. In addition to a committed lobbying office in Washington, NAWSA brought in women from home states as needed.

Such efforts, however, were too slow and uncertain for some suffragists. The style and pace of NAWSA's lobbying seemed to fit earlier times.

In 1913, young suffragist Alice Paul had led the organizing of a National March for Suffrage in Washington, D.C. While she reported to NAWSA leadership, Paul designed the event to fit her own vision and purpose. The result, held the day before Woodrow Wilson's first inauguration, was riveting and dramatic. Attacks from onlookers and limited police protection led to a congressional investigation. Paul was delighted, but NAWSA's response was more restrained.

Paul, an extraordinarily strong, strategic and committed leader, believed that only a federal amendment could ensure women their civil rights. And by 1913, some women saw NAWSA as—literally—their grandmother's organization. NWP activist Inez Irwin called them the third generation of women to demand enfranchisement and believed they were failing in that mission.[4]

THE NATIONAL WOMAN'S PARTY

Paul, Lucy Burns and other NAWSA members formed the Congressional Union (CU) to focus solely on the federal campaign.[5] In 1914, they broke with NAWSA. In 1916, they created the National Woman's Party as a parallel entity, to engage women in already enfranchised states. Meanwhile, the Women's Political Union (WPU) under Harriot Stanton Blatch was nearing success with New York state suffrage.

Blatch was a brilliant strategist, targeting wealthy society women for both funding and engagement in the fight. She recognized that making suffrage fashionable would bring in many more women. For tactics, the WPU also used very public displays such as parades and street meetings.

The WPU merged with the CU, and in 1917, all these efforts consolidated under the National Woman's Party. The WPU had brought additional membership and funding—as well as fresh workers to Washington, D.C. And Paul had a new plan. The NWP would bring the suffrage fight openly and directly to newly reelected President Wilson.

Inspired by radical British suffragettes, the NWP believed confronting politicians directly would gain publicity and force them to act.[6] Paul also had marched in a 1912 parade in New York, with an estimated eight to ten thousand people, demanding state suffrage. The protest was peaceful, and news coverage focused on prominent women who attended. Much better, from Paul's viewpoint, was the 1913 Washington march, with its news headlines about attacks on women and lack of police protection.

A police officer (*center*) arresting NWP suffragists, including Catherine Flanagan of Connecticut (*left*) and Madeleine Watson of Illinois (*right*) in August 1917. *Library of Congress.*

The NWP began an orchestrated campaign of unceasing political pressure, demonstrations and provocative civil disobedience. Recruiting primarily educated White women, it had a small army of dedicated supporters.

Image was all-important, even down to color schemes. The militant British suffragettes wore purple, white and green. NAWSA used purple, white and yellow and sometimes blue. The yellow apparently referred to the Kansas sunflower, from the organization's state campaign. Even the anti-suffragists had a color scheme: red roses, which Alice Paul joked meant they must be communists.

The NWP used purple, white and gold. And it used them so consistently that the mere sight of its banners was enough to cause arrests or detentions. For demonstrations, participants were often assigned clothing colors. White was very effective in black-and-white photography, as well as in reinforcing the idea of the women's "purity."[7]

Marches and Picketing

NWP tactics included a mix of marches, direct political lobbying, public demonstrations and hunger strikes when jailed.

Marches down Pennsylvania Avenue and gatherings at the Capitol were not new. In 1894, for instance, two major events were held. Despite a national recession, the first Labor Day parade in the city had an estimated seven thousand marchers. And "Coxey's Army," unemployed men appealing for public works funding for jobs, arrived in April. As with charges of "blocking sidewalks" used against suffragists, a charge of "walking on the grass" kept the march's leader from delivering his speech on the Capitol steps.[8]

Even hunger strikes and force-feeding had already been done. In New York, Ethel Byrne was jailed for distributing "obscene material," i.e., birth control information. In January 1917, at New York's Blackwell Island prison, she refused food and water. After eight days, she was force-fed.

But no one had yet targeted the "President's House," a home as well as an office. This most aggressive tactic began in January 1917 with NWP "Silent Sentinels." The women stood outside the White House fence holding banners demanding suffrage—at the time, an extraordinary display of boldly confronting the president to his face and in front of the world.

Even as picketing started, war preparations were underway. On the very day of Wilson's call to war, April 2, 1917, picketers were back at the White House and at the Capitol. Things went downhill from there.

Recruitment of picketers became more difficult after the war started. Many women became heavily involved in war work. And some NWP members quit the organization in opposition to wartime picketing. But still the organization found enough women to continue picketing, month after month.

Once war was declared, public support for it was generally strong. To ensure "positive" public discourse, however, Congress passed the Espionage Act of 1917 and the Sedition Act of 1918. These laws effectively stifled dissent and allowed the arrest of anyone perceived as making anti-government statements. Simply opposing the war could lead to long prison sentences.

Some people believed the NWP activities were seditious or at the least unpatriotic. The *Washington Herald* made "A Case for the Department of Justice" in a 1918 editorial: "There are hundreds of persons serving sentences in the prisons and penitentiaries of the country as a result of a great deal less unpatriotic actions than these women have taken and evidently are determined to continue."[9]

In 1894, despite a depression, the City's first Labor Day parade was held. Note the U.S. Post Office and Clock Tower under construction. *Library of Congress.*

In June 1917, NWP banners charged that President Wilson lied when he said the United States was a democracy. That triggered the first arrests of picketers, followed by jail time when they refused to pay fines. Crowds began aggressively attacking suffragists—which resulted in picketers being arrested. Banners got more sensational, and arrests continued.

Newly elected Congresswoman Jeannette Rankin speaking at the D.C. headquarters of NAWSA, 1917. She apparently did not visit the NWP. *Library of Congress.*

Jail sentences became longer. D.C. officials began sending women to the Occoquan Workhouse in Virginia. Confining Alice Paul to a hospital did not stop the effort. Nor did force-feeding, beatings and other brutal treatment of prisoners. And as other civil rights groups have found, egregious incidents can turn into beneficial public sympathy.

In the meantime, NAWSA continued its soft lobbying and focused more effort on responding to the war. This national association had a headquarters building in Washington and kept in constant touch with politicians, from Wilson on down. NAWSA leaders appealed to women to help win the war as a priority. They vehemently condemned the NWP picketing and targeting of Wilson.

The two groups disagreed on other issues, as well. NWP believed in holding the party in power—Democrats, at the time—responsible, even those members who supported suffrage. NAWSA believed in honoring members who supported the effort while working to persuade antis to change position. And the two groups were in competition for support from small circles of wealthy women.

Because of their different strategies, however, the two groups formed a powerful combination. One provoked attention in the media and political circles. The other provided a steady and familiar appeal, with strength in numbers and a respectable image. The soft lobbying of NAWSA had an estimated two million members behind it by the mid-teens. The NWP had about fifty thousand members, but they were very active. And their joint dislike of anti-suffragists was only matched by their disdain for each other.

NWP Headquarters: All for One

In line with her hyper-focus and centralized authority, Alice Paul created a hub in Washington from which all work was carried out. By 1918, this central spot was on Jackson Place, across from Lafayette Square in front of the White House.

The headquarters had multiple meeting areas, offices, a press room and a publications room. Rooms were available to rent and to house staff and volunteers. Volunteers had free room and board, while staff paid modest sums for theirs. Furnishings were donated by local supporters, so a bedroom might have a four-poster bed or a simple cot.

The NWP also had its own restaurant. The Tea Room—or "New Occoquan," in honor of suffragists who had been jailed there—was open to the public for lunch and dinner. This helped raise funds for suffrage work.

More importantly, the kitchen provided all meals to NWP volunteers and staff. This was a vital resource. People were constantly in motion: getting out newsletters and fundraising appeals, rushing to catch trains or returning exhausted from organizing trips, coming in late from picketing and lobbying, bracing for arrest while demonstrating—and on and on.

The NWP sent out a constant stream of press releases, to get stories into newspapers across the country. They often hired Harris & Ewing, a prominent D.C. photography studio, to document people and places. In 1918, newspapers were always looking for short pieces to fill their pages. They relied heavily on press releases from organizations and businesses. Coverage of suffrage varied widely, depending on the paper's editorial viewpoint.

A "special telegram," for instance, was sent to Texas newspapers by the NWP with a picture of Elizabeth holding a banner. The format personalized

The headquarters of the National Woman's Party at 14 Jackson Place NW on Lafayette Square, 1919. *Library of Congress.*

the fight for suffrage and connected a resident of the state with the fight in Washington. Elizabeth's words pushed back against those who claimed that the NWP was unpatriotic for continuing its fight for suffrage during wartime.

> *And failure to pass the amendment in this Congress means that the work of the Western campaign against the responsible party in power must be begun again this fall. We women are eager, in these stirring times, to terminate our battle for democracy here at home in order to turn the whole of our energies, with a greater sincerity and a clear conscience, toward the immense conflict waged for democracy abroad.*[10]

By the time Elizabeth arrived in D.C. in September 1918, women had been picketing the Senate, White House and Capitol for over a year. They never knew when the police might arrest them, so they always had to be ready. Two events in 1917 were particularly noteworthy.

In August 1917, the harshest banner was introduced, as White House picketers compared Woodrow Wilson to Germany's Kaiser Wilhelm. This enraged passersby, especially military personnel and war workers. They

This picture of Elizabeth with the "Mr. President, what will you do for women's suffrage?" banner was sent out in a press release. *Library of Congress.*

attacked the women, who finally withdrew to NWP's Cameron House headquarters. Sailors scaled the wall, and a bullet crashed through a window.

In November 1917 came the Night of Horrors. Ironically, the worst assaults of suffragists' multiple imprisonments and detentions occurred at Occoquan Workhouse—built as a humane alternative to brutal jails. But the head warden was frustrated by these women, who refused to respect his authority and returned repeatedly with claims of being "political prisoners." They went on hunger strikes, refused work assignments and complained to the press and politicians.

So on November 14, with thirty-one suffragists having recently arrived, the warden let guards institute a withering attack on the women. Earlier suffragist prisoners had reported facing worm-ridden food, being forced to wear filthy prison clothes and being force-fed. This time, women were still waiting to be booked when they were dragged out and thrown into cells. Assaults continued, and the warden refused them access to counsel.[11] Finally, as reports of these events were publicized outside the prison, the authorities released the prisoners.[12]

This incident was the low mark for treatment but a high mark for publicity. The NWP used the events to reinforce its message. One of the first accounts it published was that of seventy-three-year-old Mary Nolan, a small, grandmotherly figure. The image of respectable White women being carried out of prison and the horrific stories they told of their treatment helped shift public sympathy—for some. For others, these militants were criminals who could have paid their fines and avoided all this.

Several of the women involved in one or both of the 1917 incidents were still at NWP headquarters in 1918. Despite the brutal treatment, they continued to protest and face arrest. These women included little Maud Jamison; Edith Ainge, the "Angel" of NWP headquarters; and Julia Emory. During the Night of Horrors, when jailers chained Lucy Burns's arms above her head, Emory stood with her arms up in solidarity.

Picketing required a steady stream of women willing to risk abuse and jail. But the NWP could not afford to have everyone in jail or detained. Suffrage work also required people to lobby politicians, fundraise, issue press releases and publish the weekly *Suffragist*. And organizers were needed to travel out to the states, raising local support for the federal amendment. Headquarters was the base for all, both longtime workers and short-term volunteers.

In August 1918, attacks by an unfriendly crowd led to more arrests. Treatment of the women afterward, who were kept in an abandoned D.C. jail building, again provoked sympathetic publicity. Apparently as a result,

Maud Jamison of Virginia (*fourth from left*), in 1917. She endured multiple arrests for picketing. Like some others, she kept going back. *Library of Congress.*

authorities granted the NWP a permit to demonstrate in Lafayette Square on September 16. For this event, the women planned a new provocation: publicly burning Wilson's impassioned speeches on Democracy.

HIGH HOPES

On September 12, an excited young woman boarded the train in Chicago bound for Washington, D.C. Unable to find work as a writer, twenty-one-year-old Elizabeth Kalb was going to volunteer for a few weeks with the National Woman's Party in Washington, D.C.[13]

Downtown Washington, at the time, was a bustling place. In addition to business and government staff and local shoppers, returning soldiers and war workers dramatically increased the population. At the same time, an emerging flu epidemic was starting to rapidly bring down residents. News accounts began to include the number of residents who died daily from the disease.

Elizabeth's first brief letter home was written on the train and sent back with keys to her mother's luggage, taken accidently. She signed off "yours for the great Adventure," summing up the happy, nervous thrill of her journey.

Over the following months, Elizabeth wrote constantly. In part, the letters provided her suffragist mother with material for fundraising and outreach. But mostly, these are the letters of a young woman finding new independence: excited, overwhelmed at times and part of living history.

The following are her words, lightly edited. Some commentary on family and friends, for instance, has been omitted. Also, names have been corrected because Elizabeth—who wanted to be a writer—was a terrible speller! The letters provide a firsthand view of Washington life and the world of NWP suffragists.

Chapter 2

THE GREAT ADVENTURE

Friday Evening, September 13, 1918
Washington, D.C.

So! Arrived on Friday the thirteenth & put in room number thirteen, in an ancient four poster bed with a valance of *peacocks* all around it! If all that doesn't mean I'm going to jail for sure–!

The Beautiful Union Station here (with Capitol in the distance before it) presented the most stirring scene I've ever yet come across–so full of *doings*. And I thought that Chicago was crowded with soldiers & sailors, but this place is absolutely swarming with them–and of all nations. Inside of three minutes I had seen French & Italian officers, decorated; a Scotch "Lady from Hell"; wounded English soldiers and Naval & Army officers galore. In fact, our own train looked more like a troop train than anything else.

But I must say they have a fine Traveler's Aid & Information Bureau here. None of them had ever heard of Jackson Place or could tell me how to get here–or were even very sure about Lafayette Square. So I phoned & asked, then took a Mount Pleasant car [trolley] in front of the Station and arrived here at last, after tramping several blocks out of my way until I happened to catch sight of the big banner down the street. The Street had no sign.

View from Union Station, 1918. Residents, politicians, government workers, visiting dignitaries, war workers and military troops passed through the area. *Library of Congress.*

Miss Paul was the first person I saw in the office. She looks very frail. She welcomed me very heartily, saying she had met me in Houston 3 years ago & asked after you. I gave her your messages. Then she brought me up to my room, which two others are sharing with me. They are the two from the West who are mentioned & pictured in the last *Suffragist* [NWP paper]: Mrs. [Bertha] Moller from Minneapolis & Miss [Berthe] Arnold from Colorado. Neither has taken part in demonstration before. The former is rather unusual & interesting looking & young; the latter also young & *most* attractive.

I had tea with Mrs. Moller, Miss [Maud] Jamison—just a girl, in prison six weeks last October—and Miss [Vivian] Pierce of the *Suffragist*. She is *great*. But she looks like a shadow. She's got to go off the *Suffragist* next week & go into organizing & Mrs. [Clara] Wold takes over her work. She's going to turn me over to Mrs. Wold, I think.[14] Says maybe I'll write a masterpiece when I get out of jail.

The Tea Room has quite an "atmosphere" & is frequented by all sorts of people of very diverse types. Just a small room, half basement: party of naval officers at one table, some distinguished looking civilians, a scattering of army officers with their ladies— some most dainty & feminine, some affecting mannish dress.

A number of the women here have bobbed hair; Mrs. Moller and Miss Jamison have and most of them—at least a number of them—smoke cigarettes. (I wouldn't mention this to *anyone else*. E.)

Mrs. Wolf (Texas suffragist) is not here at present. About 45 or 50 are pledged for the demonstration, 25 are in the house now. A number of people seem to know of my coming as the "girl from Texas."

Whoo-ee! Wisht I had some *summer* clothes! Transfer people wouldn't promise me my trunk before Sunday.

Miss Pierce remembered a lot about your activities in Texas, engineering suffrage petitions & your work in connection with the T.F.W. [Texas Farm Women]. Asked all sorts of questions.

I'm so thrilled with everything I don't know what to do & it's all wonderful. If only you could be along! But I'm glad you're not, for it would be too much for you.

Hope I get to see something of this lovely city before I get "run in!" At present I'm going to have a nice bath in our private bathroom & crawl into bed.

With just heaps of love, Elizabeth

Saturday, September 14, 1918

I've been working all day in the banner room, sorting & listing & piling & getting ready for Monday. Covered with dirt & dead tired, so can't write much. Anyhow, I hadn't been out of the house or seen much of anybody in it.

It's easy to get Nature's Cure[15] meals here, as the servings of vegetables are so enormous. With lots of love, Elizabeth

Sunday Afternoon, September 15, 1918

It's 11:30 & I've just come up from the *Suffragist* rooms where I've been going over the files & typing some of Wilson's mellifluous phrases for use tomorrow. Berthe Arnold is saying her speech to me.

Alice Paul, 1918. *Library of Congress.*

At 8:30 we had our meeting in the ballroom and Miss Paul told us what we are to do tomorrow, down to the very last little detail, and we discussed every last possibility of going to jail and just what to do and how to conduct ourselves. I'm so thrilled I'm skeered [sic] to move suddenly for fear I blow up. Miss Paul is a *marvel.*

The line moves out at 4:30 tomorrow and the banners are all stacked and ready! First comes Mrs. Frost, leading the way with a torch. Then behind her, Vida Milholland with the American Flag, then there are to be two lettered banners used. I am to come behind Vida Milholland with "Mr. President, what will you *do* for suffrage," and then Mrs. Maury with "How long must Women wait for Liberty." Then come the four speakers: Mrs. McKaye, Berthe Arnold, Mrs. Moller and Lucy Branham. B.A. is to recite a beautiful appeal to Lafayette, written for us by Mrs. Wainwright. And at the end of her own speech Lucy Branham is to take the torch and burn the President's aforementioned utterances on "The New Freedom"— as "words, words." *That* is the big secret.

Lucy Branham of Baltimore is an unfailing wonder to me. She is so typically the pretty, soft, fluttery, very feminine Southern girl—and yet the energy of her, and the pluck, and the fire, and the things she has done! I couldn't get over my amazement.

If my trunk isn't brought up in the morning, I'll have to be fitted out with a white dress by someone, as the pageant is to be in white. The rest of them are packing away their things ready for jail. I haven't much of anything to get ready.

I was out of the house this afternoon for the first time since I arrived. Walked up around the White House grounds and back with Berthe Arnold, going to get change for the Tea Room. It's been glorious weather, but I've been too busy to poke my nose out. I've done everything today from cleaning out store room shelves to fitting electric light globes all over the building, typing lists, welcoming newcomers, tending switchboard, reprimanding recalcitrant small messenger boys, and going through *Suffragists* to pick out the sentiments for tomorrow's use.

Lucy Branham speaking to a crowd, 1919. She was part of the "Prison Special," formerly jailed suffragists describing their experiences and rallying supporters. *Library of Congress.*

The Pres. is to receive a deputation of the good little Catt Suffragists[16] tomorrow & it is just barely possible that he may use them as a dignified means of "coming across"—in which case (that is, if a date for action should be named) the demonstration would take a different form.

I think, don't you, it's time for me to go to bed....Hope to have some letters soon. With heaps of love, Elizabeth

Elizabeth wrote the following postcard to her father in Columbus, Ohio:

Monday Afternoon, September 15, 1918

Had a beautiful meeting. No disorder or unfriendly disposition on the part of the crowd. And the police *protected* us, noble creatures!

Awfully tired, so will only get word off to you so you'll know I'm not in jail or hurt. I came second in line with "Mr. Pres: what will you do for suffrage?" E.

First Public Appearance

Tuesday, September 17, 1918

I honestly don't know whether I've even got the pep to write a letter this evening or not & yet I'm so full of things to tell that I can hardly wait. And it's only six o'clock—and I'm going to stay up here where it's quiet & write to you instead of going down to supper—I'm *so* sleepy & tired. We stayed awake until 1 o'clock last night here in our room, talking and jubilating. I don't know when I've ever done so much talking before, myself. And we were all so excited that we simply could not go to sleep. We were all three of us "new," you know.

But I know you are crazy to hear all about the demonstration itself. It was wonderful. Simply wonderful. There is nothing in the world anybody could give me to make me part with the privilege of having been a part of it. It was so beautiful, so solemn, and so impressive and the spirit of it permeated even the street crowd. I can't begin to describe the feeling it gave *me*.

At 4:30 we assembled by the basement door in the alleyway at the side of the house and were given our banners. We were all in white with the satin tri-color shoulder sashes. Vida Mulholland at the last moment could not come, so young Mrs. Frost led the procession carrying the American flag. She is a lovely young woman, slim and almost ashen blonde, the wife of Lieutenant Frost of Washington, which gave us quite a bit of capital. Vida Mulholland's absence made it necessary for me to come directly after her, with "Mr. President, What Will You Do for Women's Suffrage?," and behind me was Katherine Maury with "How Long Must Women Wait for Liberty?"

Then followed in single file some 40 others bearing the beautiful purple white and gold banners. Mrs. Frost and I were both so solemnly shivery that we didn't know but we might have

Elizabeth is second in line as demonstrators march around to the Lafayette Statue, September 16, 1918. *Library of Congress.*

to be picked up somewhere on the line of march, but the inner panic evidently did not communicate itself to the hand that held the banners, because we heard numerous complimentary things along the way.

We walked, single file, very slowly, a banner pole apart, across to the edge of the park, over to the avenue, and down the avenue to the statue at the park's far end—a crowd waiting and gathering and following all the way. And at the end stood the police, waiting. And on we marched, not knowing whether we were to be arrested or rough-handled by the crowd or not. And then, in through the solemnness of it there came to me the first tiny little speck of panicky realization of what it *might* be going to mean.

But the way was cleared for us and we stepped up onto the broad plinth at the base of the statue—the flag in the center, the banners on each side and the tri-colors forming a solid mass of color all around the statue.

If the cut in next week's *Suffragist* is as good as the picture it was made from, you'll get a pretty good idea of the group—minus the color—and also a pretty good picture of me. Mrs. Wolf & I are

View of Lafayette demonstration from behind the crowd, September 16, 1918. *Library of Congress.*

Elizabeth stands center-right, behind the banner pole, September 16, 1918. *Library of Congress.*

using that one & a dandy individual of me with the banner to try to make them carry a good story to the Texas papers.

But to get back to the demonstration: we were *not* arrested. The whole meeting passed off beautifully. And it was the most *amusing* thing to see us all so solicitously protected and aided by the same policeman who had last done the arresting! Mrs. MacKaye made a good point out of that and won a big laugh from the crowd, also a sheepish one from the men themselves. "Why they're good suffragists," she said. "They've been enforced attendants at our meetings for so long that they couldn't help being converted."

No one was sure we would *not* be arrested until after Lucy Branham's "seditious" burning of the President's sacred speech was over with.

But no, the administration is clearly at the end of its string; it doesn't know *what* to do with us. And now, on top of yesterday's successful meeting, what do you think is the news today? And Mrs. Wolf & I were the bearers of it! In the face of the announcement that there would not even be called another meeting of the [Senate

Lucy Branham burns quotes from President Wilson on freedom. Elizabeth is to her right. September 16, 1918. *Library of Congress.*

Suffrage] Committee, the actual date has been set for the vote...a week from Thursday! Senator Sheppard told us.—Yessum, I've been calling on a Senator. We even called him out of the Senate session to come and talk to us.

This morning—(Next day & I can't get this finished now. I'll send on this much & rest later.) Heaps of love, Elizabeth

Wednesday, September 18, 1918

Dearest: It seems that I can hardly snatch a second's time to write & yet I know how anxious you are to hear everything & I am equally anxious to write.

I never even finished telling about the demonstration. It was positively fascinating to stand there and watch the faces in the crowd, follow the evolution of expression, in so many cases from simply amused tolerance or contemptuous curiosity to half-awakened attention, to interest, to the "By George, there's something in that!" attitude, and so on to actual enthusiasm. The first thing we knew a man sent up a twenty-dollar bill. Then tens and fives and ones began popping up all over the crowd, with amazing rapidity. Over 70 dollars came in, at a comparatively small street corner meeting.

And here was one remarkable thing about the crowd: it stayed.... When the planned program was over they weren't ready to go, so Mrs. McKaye came back and gave them some more. That woman is simply a wonder at crowd-catching speeches.

Then the kind police cleared a way for us and we marched home. It was so funny to be peered at with a sort of wondering curiosity, as if they were thinking, "Well now what kind of queer creatures are they, anyhow? They don't *look* very awful!" That's one thing about these demonstrations, they've been composed so largely of *young* women, of what would be called down South the "quality," and of always palpably refined and well educated women.[17] One man was heard to say apropos of someone, "Well, she's mighty pretty girl to be a suffragist, but I don't think I'd marry her."

So we came back, excited and rather dazed *at* coming back; back to our bags all packed for jail if need be.

And that evening [Monday] they were simply in despair in the Tea Room over the crowds, and I waited table from 6:30 to 8:30 and I got some experience! I took two tables of impatient waiters and I say!...That was a wild two hours! With 8 people all demanding different things at the same moment, and girls squabbling over orders in the kitchen! It was new and good fun though.

Volunteers Know No Rest

Texas senators Culberson and Sheppard, both Democrats, were at odds over suffrage. Culberson, the former governor, was an anti. Sheppard was a strong supporter.

Elizabeth's September 18 letter continues:

Miss Paul sent us out to call on our Senators the first thing, to find out if we could the state of things and get them to hasten things. In pursuance of his Sphinx-like policy Culberson saw no one and had no statement to make except that he had about made up his mind which way he is going to vote.

Senator Sheppard was not in his office, but we unexpectedly found his Secretary to be Sam Polk, Mrs. Wolf's one-time next neighbor, and upon introduction to me he said, "Why I know your Mother, and I've met you, I used to be in Dr. Ellis's office!" and Dr. Ellis was in the city just a few days ago and may come back to take up some government work.[18] Then we met Miss Marshall, an assistant. And when she met me she said, "Are you from Rice Institute?"–"Yes"–"Why you're the one that won that oratorical contest in Austin, weren't you? I heard you there! And you were the first girl in Texas to do anything like that," and on and on.[19]

And after lunch we went to the Senate floor and called Mr. Sheppard out, and he gave us the wonderful news [about the planned Senate vote] and was very lovely. Everyone around here is very proud of Mr. Sheppard's suffrage activities.

So I had my first view of the wonderful Capitol yesterday. And my first interview with a Senator, which thrilled me not at all.

Today I've been working on press stuff to send out to Texas & and also we went to call on some of the Texas Congressmen who had voted for Suffrage. Hatton Sumners of Dallas was the only one we found in, and he was very lovely at first when he thot we were just ordinary [NAWSA] Suffragists. But when he found we were from W.P. Hdqtrs—Ooof! He informed us that he had no use for our "outfit." Afterward he apologized very handsomely.

If the Amendment passes a week from tomorrow, there'll be nothing for me to stay for longer, because I can't afford to go into the Field Work for the winter. If it does not, why I can't tell how much longer I'd stay on in Washington, because they say that Washington is full and offering no inducements. And even if that weren't true, living is too outrageous here to make it worthwhile for a person getting even an ordinarily decent salary.

But I'm glad I came, anyway, if only for the two weeks, and helped what little I am helping, and had the experience of it all. It's worth it. I only wish I knew what I wanted to do next. I *hate* going back to Chicago to stay....

The dress & coat came today in fine shape, though I'm wondering if it wasn't rather unnecessary after all to have had so many things along, when it looks now as though everything were over but the shouting. Miss Paul said today that she feels it is almost certain to pass, Party leaders assure her of it. Senator

The press room stayed very busy, sending notices to papers around the country. NWP headquarters, circa 1919. *Library of Congress.*

Sheppard, indeed, told us it was certain to carry. Won't it be glorious to be here when it happens?

Well, goodbye, with love,

Elizabeth

Friday, September 20, 1918

This morning I went lobbying "on my own." Saw the rest of the Texas representatives who had voted "for" in the House. On the whole, I was really rather satisfied with myself! I don't think anyone would have guessed what a perfect greenhorn at the business I was, and that six months before I would have quaked in my boots at the very suggestion.

No one was unpleasant to me, though I had one long & interesting argument with Blanton (D-TX) of Abilene, who, though a suffrage supporter for years, belongs to the other party [NAWSA] and endeavored to show me the error of my ways. I actually said things, too. Oh it was really very exciting. He claims that the present possibility of immediate action is all due to the sweet, gentle, and persuasive words of Mrs. Minnie Fisher Cunningham, spoken to President Wilson last Monday.[20] Oh well, people can always "claim" and what do we care if we just get the amendment through?

Gregg (D) of Palestine says Culberson will vote against it. Blanton, Sheppard & others say he won't dare.

Miss Paul was rather interested in the statements I had to give her when I came back. I lunched with her and Miss Maud Younger, the Lobby Chairman. Miss Younger is really a wonder with the men, just the woman for her place. She's a born lobbyist, combines just the right amount of pleasing ingratiation with keen sense & political insight....

This afternoon I'm to phone all the Senators whom we know are favorable & find out if they will be on hand next Thursday. Everyone I've talked to today seems to have no idea of its not passing. There are 61 names already made public as to vote yes & Miss Younger feels almost certain of the 64. And, as she says, the White House is definitely behind this now. Even the Democratic leader would not deny that it was an Administrative measure.

Maud Younger in front of NWP headquarters, after arriving from California, December 1920. *Library of Congress.*

There's a question of it getting over with on Thursday. Miss Paul feels that if the opposition is resigned to failure it will go through quickly & if there is much delay it will show there is a determined fight to be made. We are asking our supporters not to delay action by making long speeches for it.

When I got through at the House Office Bldg, I went over to the Congressional Library [Library of Congress] and had my first peep at that marvelous place. Just stayed to get a first general impression of the building as a whole & will go back some other time for a more detailed visit. Then I wandered around the beautiful Capitol grounds for a while, and played with the squirrels, before I took a [trolley] car home.

It was raining hard when I went out this morning and is now a cold, driving rain. But at noon it had stopped a while and that's when I did my wandering. I had more fun with some squirrels, there was one bold masterful squirrel that ate peanuts out of my hand, and chased all the others away so that they were afraid for their lives to come near for their share and ran squealing in all directions. They're such funny little fuzzy-tails....

Last evening Jamie (Maud Jamison)[21] and I ran off after supper and went down on 9th St. to a picture show, which turned out to be punk. But the walk and the crowds were interesting and coming back we stopped in the Park opposite Cameron House and she told me the whole history of the riots of a year ago, and where she stood trying to haul in the flag, and where the shot was fired and where everybody was. It was thrilling.

Maud Jamison is a slight little thing with bobbed hair, is 28 & looks like a girl of 18. She's very quiet and droll and has very radical and interesting ideas. I like her immensely.

When we got back we found Berthe Arnold just back from an auto ride, during which they had had a blow out and she had had to wrestle with tires. She was starved, so we all three went down into the Tea Room, raided the pantry, resurrected some ice cream and cake left from supper, and had a lively midnight lunch before we went to bed. Nobody can get to bed before midnight in this house of incessant activity—and no one is up much before nine.

I was moved yesterday and am now down off the drawing room with Mrs. Fraher from Boston, who was afraid to stay alone. It's very nice, except that I have to go upstairs to the bathroom and I can't very often get in to get my morning & evening baths as I did before I moved.

These letters of mine don't ever really answer any of yours, do they? I have such a time getting any written at all & I know how eager you are to hear of activities here, so my times gone at that before I realize it.

Nearly 3 now & must get busy,
Your own Elizabeth

September 21, 1918

The first page has been lost, so this letter starts on page two.

The Engineers were a much better type of men anyway, quite apparently. They listened appreciatively while Mrs. Moller spoke, and every man of them bought a *Suffragist* paper when Jamie and

I went the rounds of the room. Many of the others were quite amused at the Suffragettes, and some of them were drunk, but not offensively so. We also met the engineer of the district jail, who remembered the first Prisoners and who was most denunciatory of their treatment. Finally, we came pattering and sloshing back through the rain after a trip in a jammed up streetcar. On the whole, it was most decidedly *quite* a new experience.

Today is clear but still quite cold. After breakfast I dodged out from under the Eagle Eye of A.P. [Alice Paul], as everyone calls her, and hiked it over back of the White House & around the mile circle in front of the Monument, then over past the Treasury Building to a drug store for soap & films & back by the park, briskly. And I felt most gorgeous after it. Then I got busy phoning Senators again. Did I tell you that yesterday most of them answered something like this: "You bet he will!" "I sure will be there!" "I'm a sure thing if I'm still alive!" etc. etc. I still have a few to get that I couldn't reach before.

⌒

This letter doesn't look so very terribly much as though I had been stopping every 2 seconds to wrestle with nickels & dimes & five-dollar bills, now does it, or jumping up to open the door or smile upon & soothe impatient diners or see that everyone had menus & pads.

And now Miss Paul has just told me that I am to phone all the *rest* of the Senators—opposed & all. So I see my afternoon's work laid out for me.

Don't you ever worry about my starting on *coffee (or cigarettes)!* I *guess not!* Do you think I have suddenly lost what intellect I was ever possessed of, to have had my summer's work make no more impression on me than that? The idea!

Also I am taking every possible care of myself. When I reach the tired point and work still obtrudes itself, as it has a way of doing in this place, I just politely ignore it and slide out for a breath of air in the park or a run around the block. You can't hide by going to bed, because if there's anything to be done the Eagle Eye above referred to pursues you everywhere within the sixteen walls of the place.

It's wonderful to work *with* Miss Paul when your heart's in the same cause with hers. But I wouldn't work *for* her for any nameable salary. I'd be dead inside six months. She's *awful*. Indefatigable herself, nothing escapes her, however small, and she drives everyone else around her at the same pace that she goes herself....

Haven't got down to the office to look for mail yet today. Yours coming yesterday was mighty welcome. I haven't even seen the papers more than once or twice since I came, no time to read them & I have no idea what the war news is. I hate not to keep up & I think I'll make a point of doing it regardless, from now on. The *Tribune* publicity was dandy.

Time to get busy now, so goodbye... How you must hate these scrawly, penciled letters of mine! But it's the best I can do.

Heaps of Love,
Elizabeth

Monday, September 23, 1918

Dear Folks: It's almost supper time & I've just been for a walk to warm up & am now sitting in the sun over in the park, endeavoring to get a note off to you.

I have been sitting at the addressograph steadily all afternoon and have handled something over 1,700 envelopes—the envelopes that we have are to carry the good news out to all *Suffragist* subscribers after next Thursday [day of the Senate vote].

The news this a.m. was that the amendment was *not* to come up as stated—postponed. But at 12 o'clock when Senate convened, Sen. Jones of the Committee stated on the floor that the press had no basis for their announcement & that it most surely *would* come up.

A bunch of us had gone over to the Capitol. Miss Younger to see the managers, a little but very sprightly South Carolina girl & I to "do" the South, Mrs. Moller, Katherine Maury, Berthe Arnold, Clara Wold & others taking other sections.

We had some very amusing interviews with Anti's. For much as we would explain that this was not a lobby visit, some of them would insist on arguing. One SC man's chief reason for opposing the

Amendment is that it was first introduced by Susan B. Anthony & she was an abolitionist! Therefore all American women, including all Southern women, should for all time be denied suffrage. This was Wanamaker, Sen. Smith's Secretary. When we mentioned it as an Administration measure, he admitted that he did not feel called upon to agree with the Admin in everything. I told him that in time of war some people would call that rank treason.[22]

While we were there Smith (D-SC) came in, raging like a mad bull because the question of fixing a minimum price for cotton is being agitated and even suggested as an Admin [War] Measure. And the rumors had already affected the market to an alarming extent.

It is rumored that Smith is unalterably against us, Benet (D-SC) *may* vote for us. Oh how funny it all is, anyway, these cautious changings & these careful approaches from men whose convictions (if they have such things) you know have not altered in the slightest. And then they say that nothing can make them vote other than their conscience dictates!

For instance, Senator Robinson (D-AR) is as much interested in the success of the Amendment next Thursday as we are ourselves—so he told us today. And Miss Younger says that a year ago he was most malevolently opposed. His Secretary says he "owes a debt to the women."

Just a week today since the demonstration. And it seems as though I've lived a month since I came!

Yesterday [Sunday] I "laid off." I had been phoning Senators the day before until I felt as though I should grow to the telephone. In the morning Mrs. Fraher & I tried to have a fire in our grate & smoked ourselves out. Found afterward that the flue was choked up, so we can have no fire.

We nearly freeze in that place. Have to come outside to get warm. Inside it's as drafty & damp as a barn—a poorly built barn. These huge old houses are lovely in summer—but! And as yet we have no coal. It will be enough of a proposition to keep the place heated even after the furnaces get started.

Yesterday morning I got off ten *Suffragist* letters & sample copies. After Mrs. Fraher & I vanished before we got presented with jobs, and took a lovely brisk walk in the sunshine, over past the Art Gallery, the Pan-American and Continental Buildings, the Navy

Drawing for the *Suffragist* by NWP artist Nina Allender, 1914. *Library of Congress.*

building, and down to the Potomac, then up to the Monument. That wonderful shaft fascinates me. You can always see the top of it above the trees, veiled and mysterious—looking, or else the whole of it, sharply outlined and gleaming in the sunlight. We sat for a while there on the mound and watched it, catching the new fascination that it has close up, when you get all its immensity.

Then we came down to the Circle and listened to the Marine Band for a while until time to come home for supper. I was too cold and uncomfortable to write letters last evening, too cold to do anything but crawl into my cot.

Mrs. Fraher is another interesting one, surely. She is Irish, so very Irish, born in Ireland but a real American now. And she is by conviction a Sinn Féiner (Shinn Faner, she calls it). It's interesting to know one at close range, and I must confess that when you hear her side of it you don't feel so unqualifiedly sure of your censure.[23]

Her brother has been in jail, forcibly fed and hunger-striking for 3 months. She says Ireland is simply one big garrison of English troops. She says of *course* they don't want Home Rule. The only ones that want Home Rule are the planter class of the North of Ireland, not real Irish people at all. What they want is *Independence*, the same as America fought for in '76. As for "Tay Pay" O'Connor, she says he don't dare set foot in Ireland. There's a lot of intensely interesting things that she's said that I haven't time to write about, but I'm enjoying learning all I can, hearing the other side....

I'm going to have to run now or I won't get any dinner. Here's my day's menus: Breakfast—baked apple, orange. Noon—string beans, boiled onions, waldorf salad, bran muffins, baked apple and cream. Night—mashed potatoes, corn on cob, turnips, tomato salad, Lemon Blanc Mange.

The Salads are very nice and the portions unusually large.

Farewell my dears for now.

Elizabeth

Playing Hooky at Mt. Vernon

Tuesday, September 24, 1918

What a lovely, lovely day I have had! I played hooky! Mrs. Fraher and Miss James were going to Mt. Vernon [George Washington's estate, restored by the Mt. Vernon Ladies Association, across the Potomac River and south, in Virginia], and it was such a lovely day that I couldn't bear to stay indoors, so I succumbed to their urgings, and up and went along. We went on the electric [streetcar], making an hour's ride, and we got some apples and grapes and peanuts and dates and took [them] along, and went out into the woods and had them for lunch.

I can't begin to tell you what an impression that place made on me; but you've been there so perhaps you know, but not unless you saw it as unhurriedly and "uncrowdedly" as I did. There is the most all-pervading sense of peace over it all.

Nothing that ever has been or could be said or written about it, no painting, no photograph, could ever begin to describe the place or do it justice, could ever paint it as it appeared to me in the sunlight of a glorious day in autumn, with flecks of color through the woods, and lovely purpled vistas across river and distant hills.

The sudden glimpses through openings in the woods, down past old ivied brick walls to a bit of shimmering water; the softly rounded turn of a green hill, with misty stretches of knoll on knoll in the distance; a curving, hedged-in road, opening unexpectedly onto a sheer bluff yellow with golden rod, and the wide stretch of peaceful river below; rolling green lawns framed round in great oaks, with a trail of weeping willow down to the water's edge; and always and always a new scene of beauty opening up around every curve, at the top of every knoll, from every door and window and angle of the house itself. I could have stayed on forever.

And all this is just the estate itself, which to me is the most ideal in situation, in the placing of house and gardens, that could ever be anywhere....

I feel like a new person for my whole day spent out in the hills & the glorious air & sunshine, so glad to get away from the damp, chill house out into the invigorating warmth and coolness of sun and wind.

Reached home a little before six, stopping to leave some films to be developed....Now I'm going up for a sitz bath & pop into bed.
Heaps of love,
Elizabeth

DIRTY POLITICS

Friday Morning, September 27, 1918

Well, our long-awaited day is over and nothing has happened, just as Miss Paul thought it would. She said the night before, after she had returned from a long séance[24] of seeing personally some doubtful ones, that she felt sure it would not come to a vote at least until today. Now we don't think the debate will be over until tomorrow; and we don't very much care, because it looks as though we were one vote short. Sad but true, and apparently no hope for it. Johnson (R-CA) was called home on account of serious illness to his family, can't be back. And of course you know, Senator Gallinger's (R-NH) successor is a rabid anti.

The galleries were jammed and packed yesterday. We went up at 10:30 and sat until 5, taking each a little bundle of sandwiches and some fruit to keep us from starving. There were about a hundred or more in our section. In the gallery opposite us sat the very proper and self-righteous National Americans [NAWSA] each with her pretty little yellow paper rose. Across in the other direction sat the boxful of Antis with their red boutonnieres (and our dear friend the Senator Wadsworth (R-NY), on the floor, wearing one also).

We had a secret service man planted in our gallery to see that nothing violent was promulgated from our vicious midst. And the old doorkeeper who had charge of us was a perfect fiend— but he enjoyed his taste of authority so much that we couldn't begrudge it him. If anyone rose in their seat to lean over and speak to someone (this of course was in the hours before the Senate even convened), he was on the spot to blusteringly tell them to "set down or he'd *make* 'em." He took away newspapers and paper and pencils and bags that looked too big and possibly dangerous—

Puck

WOMAN

"Queen of the Home," say the Anti-Suffragists—
Yes; Queen of a Cook-Stove Throne.

Left: Answer to antis: "Queen of the Cook-Stove Throne." Kenneth R. Chamberlain, artist. *Puck* magazine, 1914. *Library of Congress.*

Opposite: The original warning card handed to Elizabeth in the balcony of the Capitol, September 27, 1918. *Handy/ Marshall Collection.*

and endeavored to browbeat everybody generally. He was a scream. Then the accompanying little slip of paper was distributed among us in large numbers. Wasn't it rich? Poor things, they never feel quite safe, never know what we may spring next, even in our most peaceful moments.

After the Senate did convene, time dragged interminably while the precious Elders of our Nation argued and vilified and perorated, each one before a group of empty or might-as-well-have-been-empty Senatorial seats. Vardaman (D-MS), he of the long grey locks, made the first speech, favoring the F.S.A. [Federal Suffrage Amendment] and drawing most of his arguments from the ancient Spartans and Greeks. All of the speech-making with

NOTICE.

Demonstrations of approval or disapproval by the occupants of the galleries are forbidden by a rule of the Senate.

Persons violating this rule will be ejected.

By order of the Committee on Rules:

CHARLES P. HIGGINS,
Sergeant at Arms.

the exception of one was confined to Southern Democrats. Owen (D-OK, Cherokee) made the only real Suffrage speech as *was* a speech, and his was very short and to the point, asking for action and the cessation of all this hashing and re-hashing pro and con that everybody had been perfectly familiar with for ages. One Kansas man made a really good speech too.

Hardwick—I think it's Hardwick—(D-GA) made an eloquent appeal against federal action, using all the dear old familiar arguments. The opponents, strange to say, are nearly all in favor of Suffrage, warm espousers of the cause on behalf of dear defrauded Woman, or else they have "nothing to say" of the merits or demerits of Suffrage: it is to them purely a matter of *method*.

And then out comes a pro and says in that sweet way peculiar to the Administration, "BUT we must remember that our Great Leader, our Beloved President, who has led us to victory in so many measures, has *asked us* to regard this a war issue, and to help in this way to make the world safe for democracy!" Oh the irony of it! The deliciousness that makes you boil and writhe—and crumple with laughter!

Yes, States Rights really held sway; but the chief spectacle in that connection was OHIO in the person of our respected Senior Senator hiding behind that Sovereignty of the State junk, and swelling up visibly with righteous indignation at the thought of any one asking *him* to call upon *his* state to submit to Federal dictation!

Oh Lord! Why dwell on it? It was rotten—the whole of it. There were not three sincere men among our pro speakers, unless it be Sheppard and Owen and Sheppard did not speak. But if one such session of our great Congress is not enough to impress you with the peanutness of our lawmaking body, then a person so unimpressed must be very pachydermatous as to skin.

We are going back today—and hear some more twaddle. And probably tomorrow the great Protectors of Womankind will have their way in safeguarding the female and the HOME from the slime of politics and in preserving the States from being obliged to submit to the decision of the majority.

Those men are such perfect *dubs*! They aren't even informed about ordinary points of constitutional law and history. They tangle each other all up shamefully until no one is sure where he is, and they use nothing but worn out arguments that must surely have flourished in Noah's day. Any Woman's Party Member I know could have made a more intelligent and convincing speech, either for *or* against. And oh golly! What some of our *real* speakers could have done to 'em!

Well, I shall not recess until after the afternoon's session, and then write some more.

Evening

I've talked so much about it all since I came back from the Senate this afternoon that I can't even write about it now. It's all gone out of me. I've boiled dry. I'll just have to go to bed now & trust to writing in the morning. But if I do that, something is sure to happen & then nothing will get written at all.

The session was the most disgraceful thing I ever dreamed possible anywhere. I simply seethe with rage every time I think about it. And yet the outcome was really to our advantage, since it put off the final issue another day in this most critical time & since it showed to us the way the Democrats are trembling in their boots on account of the possibility of a Western Campaign.

Pittman (D-NV) started it by making a most sensational charge upon the Republicans, saying almost with tears that they had fixed it so that no matter what happened the Democrats would be blamed. The R's, he said, have pledged ½ the votes necessary to pass the Amendment, giving ⅔rd of their own voting strength, so making it plain that if the Amendment came to vote & was defeated the responsibility would be with the D's, who refused to furnish the other necessary votes out of a very much larger number. And if the vote were *not* taken, they could say, because of the same D majority, that the D's had refused to let it come to a vote. So the D's were condemned before the people in any event, because the R's knew perfectly well that the necessary votes were lacking at this time.

Now Pittman is one of our supporters & he charges that the R's are responsible for forcing the measure now, *knowing* that it cannot carry & satisfied to let it be killed so that that failure can be laid before the people as a *Democratic* failure before election time.

He & Smoot (R-UT) [25] had one glorious scrap, during which the Woman's Party got slammed from both sides & each side accused the other of trying to kill or delay the passage of the amendment. Pittman, poor man, was in desperation & quoted whole pages from recent issues of the *Suffragist* to prove the threatened annihilation of the Dem. Party & to prove that the N.W.P. is in cahoots with the R.'s & that now the R.'s are betraying their trust as they betrayed the trust of Dem. Suff. Supporters in the Senate. Oh it was rich! What a wonderful advertisement for the "*Suffragist.*" Pittman really said everything an N.W.P. could have said except "Please subscribe." But to see them wail at each other & tear their hair!

Next scene on the program, a duel between Reed (D-MO) & J. Ham [Lewis] (D-IL, Majority Whip).

Reed took the occasion of Pittman's partisan charges to rail about the disgraceful state of affairs when such things as Suffrage could be made pure politics in the Senate. And he said horrible things about "female lobbyists" and "petticoat bosses" and the "senate's shame," and on and on and on. And J. Ham sprang to the defense of the ladies. It certainly was a drawn-sword encounter, and they were good rivals, equally skilled in damning eloquence and sneering politeness and well-veiled insults.

Of course Reed had the last word and enjoyed himself for some thirty minutes calling the "distinguished Senator" a liar and a few other less mild epithets. Also he said he scarcely knew how to defend himself from such an attack. "When a man comes at you with doubled up fists," said he, "you know what to do. But when he comes with a flutter of lace and delicate notions, and the aroma of sweet perfumes assail your nostrils, you don't know whether you're expected to assail him or embrace him." And more disgusting and keenly barbed conversation of a like nature, dragging in all sorts of irrelevant matter personal and private to J. Ham.

And *then* came his real attack on the Woman's Party. For a solid hour he raved and ramped and vilified and slandered, secure in the knowledge that no one can be held accountable for anything he says on the Senate floor. He accused the Party as a whole of every conceivable crime of disloyalty and sedition and singled out special individuals for special attack. In the beginning it was made to seem like an unintended outburst of indignation brought on by what Pittman had said about politics, but it was evident that the whole attack was carefully planned beforehand, because he was well-fortified with a stack of papers.

The most dastardly part of the whole thing was when he accused Hazel Hunkins[26] ("and you all know *Hazel's* part in the Suffrage campaign," he sneered) of having "cursed the American flag," called her a common jailbird, read statements made by District jailers to that effect, and told how "*The Woman Patriot*," the paper which originally attacked the Picket prisoners, had endeavored to drag Miss H's name into some other disgusting insinuations. Walsh of Montana, Miss H's Senator, sprang up to protest, saying that he *knew* her personally and he knew that the statements were untrue and that Reed had no right to bring up the matter without stating Miss H's reply to the matter.

Reed said very smoothly that he had intended to lay both sides fairly before the Senate, but it was evident he had had no such intention, for it took about 15 minutes for him to find the telegram which Miss H. had sent the "*Patriot*"

Hazel Hunkins, circa 1917.
Library of Congress.

enjoining them from printing their slanderous accusations on pain of suit for damages.

"But," he said, "denials are sometimes very easy to make. And actions speak for themselves. Anyone belonging to a group that would profane a public park and a sacred statue by a demonstration against the *chief magistrate of this country*, would be quite equal to saying, 'God damn the old American flag.' The two are practically synonymous."

To *think* that a man (so-called) can get up on the floor of the United States Senate and rave in that manner for hours without there being any way of stopping him! And to think that a person could be allowed to say the things he said!

Most of the others have got fairly used to such things by this time, but for me—I simply saw red. I was so furious I could hardly sit still. It seems so *intolerable* that we should have to sit helpless and let such impressions as any beast may choose to promulgate go out and, of course, be accepted all over a country that has no other means of knowing. Oh well.

—

The afternoon closed with a delightful peroration read by Thomas (D-CO) and addressed to those angels, the National Suffrage Association [NAWSA], "perfect ladies," who "never mixed in politics," who had striven so long "in their sweet and gentle way," etc., etc., etc., ad impossibilum. Whenever I can forget Reed long enough I remember the exciting afternoon with great joy.

I must stop now & send this off. I'll try & answer your dear letters when I write of tomorrow's séance. Lovingly your daughter.

Sunday, September 29, 1918

Last evening I had to keep the cash box in the Tea Room & then went out to get a walk before going to bed so I didn't get to write then.

But there was nothing to write of concerning the Senate session. The afternoon dragged interminably, with a brief continuation of the Pittman-Smoot controversy to begin with. In spite of my

Republican leanings I will say that personally Pittman impresses me a little and Smoot not at all.

Smoot is one of those smooth, oily, pious-looking kind of men that make you instinctively wary, and if he's been in charge of the Republican maneuvers in this matter, why I wouldn't be willing to swear by the innocence of the party in regard to this charge. Of course, the Democrats *are* responsible, as the party in power, for the failure to grant suffrage long ago, but Pittman is most plainly worried over the present failure.

But what a huge joke it is to think of the way the insignificant, powerless, "petticoat politicians," the Women's Party, who are (registering indignation) "in *no way* responsible" for the burning issue of Suffrage today and for the worried state in which the Democrats find themselves, to think of the way in which this "*little* group of selfish, neurotic women," with an organization "reaching its fangs into every township and every county and every state of our union" (statements quoted from the same gentleman), is occupying the attention of that dignified body, the Senate of the United States of America!

Isn't it rich, this admission of theirs concerning our importance, what a factor they regard us?

The rest of the afternoon, interrupted frequently by interposed discussions on other matters, very obviously interposed & stretched out for a purpose, was given over to a long peroration by well-meaning but stupid Shafroth (D-CO). Some of his points were very good for a general discussion on the merits of Suffrage, but they had little or no bearing on the points of objection in the present situation.

Oh yes & another of our hopes committed suicide at the beginning of the session. Benet (D-SC),[27] who had made no state of intentions, but who had seemed in a receptive & favorable frame of mind & who had been among those [that] both sides accepted as our property, rose to remove all doubts concerning his position. He had been waiting, he said, for someone to convince him that it was a War Measure & no one had yet made that plain to him & considering his constituency, he could vote for the measure on no other grounds. Therefore he would cast his vote against it.

Things look quite hopeless, unless there should be some unlooked-for chance by special intervention by the President before Monday. If the vote is taken Monday & it fails, we will protest in a demonstration on the Capitol steps. What will happen then no one knows.

Monday Morning

We are trying awfully hard now to raise some extra money to meet coal bills for Headquarters this winter. In the tearoom we have an artistic poster saying "It Will Cost Three Dollars a Day to Keep Us Warm this Winter. Won't you Warm the Cause for One Day?" We've had no heat yet and the house is awfully cold & clammy.

Evening

I was sitting calmly in the Park up to this point, writing away, when Clara Wold went by to the [street] car, saw me, dashed back and said, "Haven't you heard the news? The President is to address the Senate at 1 o'clock. You'll have to hurry down if you want to get a seat!" So very precipitately I dashed over to the house and into my coat and hat and over to the Capitol. We had the news at 10 o'clock, way in advance of the papers.

And the President *did* address the Senate. Heavens! What a thrilling occasion! It seemed, looking back a few months, almost too remarkable to be true! And the speech itself was a wonder, and so feelingly delivered. If you hadn't known a few amusing facts, if you could have believed that it came, unprompted, from the depths of his heart, you could have loved him for it. As it was, he accomplished it very gracefully and graciously and with a quiet, simple dignity that must have been rather hard to maintain, considering his peculiar situation in the matter.[28]

A brief, dramatic fifteen minutes and then the crowds left and the noble Senators resumed their diatribes quite unaffected (?) by it all. Of course, they cannot capitulate immediately. After debating for three days, they could not immediately and with dignity succumb under less than *one* more day.

Reed, Martin, Benet & others looked most perturbed.

Phelan (D-CA) made one *real*, splendid, ringing speech for the measure, the first that really answered any points, and the first with the courage to champion & give credit to N.W.P. methods.

I'll send this much along now....I'm utterly worn out now, so goodnight. Elizabeth

The next day, October 1, Elizabeth was at the Senate for the amendment's roll call vote. Despite Wilson's speech and support, the amendment failed to pass.

Sick with Waiting—or with Flu?

Wednesday Afternoon, October 2, 1918

I've been sitting here in the park taking a sun bath & trying to persuade myself that I felt like writing some letters. But I think if I write a line or two to you I will be doing well.

I came back from the Senate yesterday afternoon and aches and pains! *Half* the people in the house have come down one after another with a bad cold—due I think to the confinement these past few days in the very close, bad air of the Senate, with irregular meals and a cold, damp house at nights. Our coal has been coming in today, so maybe that last will be remedied.

I had eaten nothing but fruit during the day—so I had that in my favor—except for a glass of milk before I went up to the Capitol at eleven. Had prunes, banana and orange for breakfast. Last night I ate nothing, but exercised to warm up, bathed and massaged my eyes, which had been hurting for a couple of days, sniffed water up my nose, put compress on my throat, packed myself up in a trunk pack,[29] and put myself to bed with all the blankets, coats, and sweaters I could find and a hot water bottle at my freezing feet.

My room opens off the ballroom and while I didn't get to sleep until after twelve because some people were dancing, still I was warm and I could rest and doze a little. Later in the night and until morning I was pretty uncomfortable, with racking pains and alternate hot and cold flushes and dizziness. But the pack did its work, and today I have felt much better. The only bad pain is in my head, and in my chest now. There's no "cold in my head" at all, just a rather deep and bothering cough. Tonight I'll try a Scotch pack for that, as my throat doesn't seem to be sore.

This morning I got up and bathed my eyes and had a cold splash and went back to bed again. Miss Small got me a fresh hot water bottle for my feet, and Miss James got me oranges, and I've had just dilute orange juice twice today. I slept some this morning and noon time, and about three I dressed and came out in the Park for sun and air, which is making me feel much better. I think another night of packs and another day of juice will fix me up all right. People think I'm killing myself with cold water and nothing to eat to strengthen me. I've been away from it so long that it seems awfully funny to hear people say in all seriousness and solicitude— "Oh, but you *must* eat something!"

Just so the authorities don't take it into their heads that I'm coming down with "Spanish Influenza," this new "contagious" disease that is scaring everyone to death now, and rush me off to the hospital to be quarantined and "doctored" as they are doing with every suspicious case.

⌒

In spite of the defeat yesterday, Miss Paul is really feeling very much elated at the remarkable trend of events. The partisan fight on the floor, wherein each party sought with so much feeling to shift responsibility to the other; the fact of the President's feeling impelled to address the Senate on the matter, for the first time since the days of Washington and Jefferson, it is said; the speech that he made, ringing with every phrase that she has been laboriously teaching him these many months; Cummin's vindication of Party tactics & lastly the perfectly marvelous statement made in last night's *Star* [newspaper] by David Lawrence, Administration mouth piece, entitled "The Doom of Democratic Party Control." You'll doubtless see it in the Chicago papers, as it's syndicated stuff. He's the author of the article you sent me several years ago. Just think of the tremendous amount she [Alice Paul] has accomplished! The energy and force and resourcefulness of her is simply amazing, isn't it?

There's to be a National Executive Council meeting tonight to determine future action. Immediately, here in Washington, it may take the form of picketing the Senate steps. No one of us knows what the next few days may bring forth. I've *got* to get to feeling well at once.

I'll not send this until tomorrow when I know one way or another how I come out of this, no use worrying you uselessly & I think there's little doubt but that I'll be all right. I guess I have now did my best & I'll just sit here & watch people the rest of the time until the sun goes down. Heaps of love, Elizabeth

Next Day, October 3

Not any better today, have been very feverish especially my head. No rest last night....Hate sending this to you like this, as will doubtless be well by the time it reaches [you], but you'll probably worry if you don't hear. Have stayed in bed all day today...sleeping fitfully but shoveling coal in alley just outside my window not specially conducive thereto.

Saturday, October 5, 1918

Just a note following [tele]gram, to let you know how I am. I have gone through the five stages of inflammation most beautifully, in as many days. Thursday was certainly the period of Destruction, with a *great big D*, but in the night the fever broke and there followed yesterday the period of Abatement, with today, Reconstruction.

I had a glorious fever to gladden the heart of a Nature Cure and make an ordinary person tremble with dread. Thanks be that I was not so far out of my head as not to be able to fight strenuously against having a doctor and didn't let anyone know how bad I really was or I fear my fight would have been in vain.

It was the burning-up-est fever I ever remember having. I had all sorts of weird hallucinations all Wednesday and on Thursday I dozed fitfully all day, never quite sure if I were asleep or not or whether I was awake or not.

Of course, as I told you, I was very achey and feverish all over my body, but my head was the worst. It felt swelled to about twice normal and was one big ball of fire and pain. One of my brilliant ideas of the night was to get hold of a bucket of water so as to save the rest of me if my head went up in smoke. My mouth, gums, and throat were afire in the same way, and my eyes so swollen and inflamed and bloodshot that I could not look at anything or keep them open long at a time. Since the fever broke they are much better and incidentally, all the skin is cracking and coming off my face like checked varnish. Even up around the edge of my eyes....

Have been pretty weak and sore since fever left, of course, but that's better than aches. Sore throat about gone, by yesterday. Was troubled by a day's croupy cough that felt like it came all the way up from my diaphragm and nearly broke me in two each time without raising anything....

The other poor people, with their doctor and nourishing food, are still sick; but I can't make any impression on them. Broke my fast today on an orange for breakfast, a pear for lunch, and a lettuce salad for supper.

You should have seen the flesh roll off me in those few days, just literally burned up. Hip, rib, collar and cheek bones again asserting themselves prominently. I imagine I'll gain it back rapidly though.

People have been very good to me and have looked after me as much as could be expected in this busy household, but I'll confess that I've wished *once* or *twice* that I might have my own folks around–yes–honestly! I'm very proud of the way I handled my case, tho, in spite of being "dippy" half the time.

Miss Paul got back from NY only this morning, with $5,000 in contributions. Isn't that wonderful? No one has yet heard any inkling of plans. I'm so glad nothing "came off" this weekend, because I'll be all right and ready for anything by Monday....

I think the telegrams [likely rallying supporters] you got out was a splendid piece of work. But I wished after had sent you the wire that had not done so, for feared you would overdo yourself, just as you did....Here each one of us sent out wires (5 or 6 of us), wrote out our own wire with signature & appended a list of 60 or more names that that wire was addressed to & the boy came & got the bunch....

Heaps of love, Elizabeth

Monday Morning, October 7, 1918

If it hadn't been for Maud Jamison yesterday would have been my downfall, I'd have turned into just a little old homesick baby. The day before, feeling so well I had tried to get up and found my legs made of soft dough and my head of feathers, which was rather discouraging. And Julia Emory and Nita Pollitzer had both come down that day with it, in the next two rooms to mine. And that evening Nita was weeping in a heap on her cot the other side of the partition. And on Sunday I felt like a lost sheep, in my dismal room. It was rainy and dark.

In p.m. the sun came out & Jamie came and got *me* out and took me into the lovely park to sit on a bench and fill myself full of warm fresh air and watch the people go by. And I felt lots better. Condition in lung region still pretty bad. But I feel so wonderfully better ever since the fever left that I hardly feel I can say I'm sick anymore.

If this *is* the thing they call Spanish Influenza, then I'll have to admit that it really is different from any grippe or cold I ever had. The way it gets hold of you way down deep in your lungs and wrenches and pulls like it wants to get 'em out by the roots had me scared. And that orful pain in the small of the back, and the way my head was—

I hope you got my letter written Saturday, tho' I have some fears of its being lost. Someone else gave it to the 'phone operator to stamp & she is very careless & irresponsible.

A very funny menstrual flow began yesterday, a week and a half ahead of time, which has not contributed to my comfort in any way.

I really feel very lucky though about throwing off the disease so quickly. Miss Younger is still in bed and so is Miss [Wold], Kate Heffelfinger went home but was still very sick. Julia Emory and Nita Pollitzer are both very bad, Mrs. Moller and Berthe Arnold are both getting down, and Doris Stevens' case developed into double pneumonia, very severe. She was moved out of the house. Only two people, who were down with it before I was, have gotten quite well so far.

Same Day, Evening

I have spent the whole afternoon getting arrested. Why the whole afternoon, you say? The trouble was, we didn't *stay* arrested.

Just before Senate convened at 12:00 an automobile containing Miss Paul, three banners & four girls well bundled up in wraps, left Headquarters and sped up the Avenue to the Capitol plaza, depositing its burden at the foot of the Senate steps.

At the top of the flight two girls stood stretching the huge white and gold "We Demand—" banner across the center of the entrance, while on either side a picket [held] a purple, white and gold banner on a pole. The strong north wind tugged and pulled and strained at them enviously.

For about 5 minutes they stood there. Then, a Lieutenant of the Capitol Police appeared in the offing, approached, and told them it was against the rules to display any flag other than the American flag on the Capitol grounds, and advising them to move over onto B St., opposite the Senate Office Bldg. No one moved or replied. The officer went away. Presently two more appeared, repeated the announcement with a few threats, walked all around us, and went away. Fifteen minutes of peace ensued.

Then there appeared a burly individual out of the building who jerked the banners violently from our hands and marched us inside, down through subterranean passages to the Sergeant's office. There one fatherly old man read us lectures and gave us kindly advice while the grim individual looked on grimly and the four culprits, enjoying the nice warm room, said nothing. After ten minutes or so our banners were locked up, and we were escorted out to the open air where, across on the stone coping, sat Miss Paul and Mrs. Boecket and Mrs. Baker waiting for us.

We then made haste homeward, tacked more banners on a larger supply of poles, loaded them into the taxi, climbed in and returned. This time, only two, bearing one big banner between them, ascended the steps. Almost five minutes elapsed before the banner was torn from hands and they came down empty handed. Vivian Pierce and I were waiting in the parked auto across the way, and both of us immediately hopped out, took 2 tricolors and made for our objective. We got clear to the top of the steps and took our stand before [we were] interfered with and then we refused to give up our banners and were marched downstairs once more to the Sergeants office.

Here we sat comfortably for the better part of an hour, while a mighty confab took place on the outside concerning us. We had been joined shortly by the other two with two more banners. The old chaps were awfully nice to us, told us what good Suffragists they were and how they hated to be rough to us and hated to see us injuring our Party like we were, etc. etc., and advising us to "light into [Senator] Benet of S.C., he's the one that double-crossed us."

Finally they took our names again, locked up the rest of the banners and once more escorted us back to Miss Paul and the waiting taxi. By this time the Senate had adjourned (until next Thursday), so we all climbed into our car and drove off, the officers assembled to bid us farewell—until Thursday.

Now we're back and I must stop, for I have to take poor miserable Berthe Arnold's place in the Tea Room.

Yours & Father's letters came today. Will try & answer later. Let's go to California next! E.

Nothing Stops the Work

Tuesday, October 8, 1918

Dearest Mother,

Today is still colder but bright & sunny and I have chosen the warmest place I can find—a sunny corner of the Park. I feel no ill effects of my expedition yesterday, tho last night my chest was a little more painful & it hurt clear around into my back when I coughed. But this morning it's no worse than usual.

One of the queer things about this business is the way it affects your heart. While I was sick I could feel that my pulse beat very slowly & after I got up & was able to wriggle around, even two or three steps up was enough to start things pounding laboriously. Now the least start, excitement or exertion leaves my skin quite bloodless & me quite breathless.

Miss Paul had a doctor, Miss Rosenberg, in to look us all over last evening & she was scandalized that I should have gotten out of bed yesterday so soon & ordered me to go very slowly, lie down frequently during the day & not do much climbing of stairs.

In her advice to the others she made no mention of medicines or anything but rest & quiet, "withdrawal" of heavy food as Dr. Ulmer would say & keeping bowels open.

⌒

Alas, I have some sad news to impart. The silk sleeves to my serge have completely gone to pieces, in folds at elbow first, then over the shoulder, so I can only wear it about the house under my sweater. I am so bereft because now I have to wear my brown regularly instead of specially. And it's a good bit lighter weight for one thing & it doesn't look so nice with my grey coat & black hat for another. But such is life....

It was such a bad day no pictures were taken yesterday.... It is very truly fall here now. Yesterday's strong wind very much depleted the supply of leaves on the trees, but everything is still very beautiful....Don't you think it would be nice for us all to go to California for the winter? Maybe I could get into newspaper work out there & make it permanent.

I have to go to the bank now & get change & be in the Tea Room after lunch, so will have to stop now. "Us and the Senate" are having a recess until Thursday, so there's nothing doing *until* then, but we don't know what may *be* doing then. You know they *could* have given us $100.00 fine or 60 days for yesterday, had they been so minded.

Lots of love, Elizabeth

Wednesday, October 9, 1918

Dear Mother,

You'd probably scold if you knew what I've been doing today. Been down in the basement on the cold cement floor, tacking banners onto poles. It couldn't be helped—we are so short of people now, with nearly everybody sick & the banners had to be got ready for tomorrow. I sat out in the Park though for an hour after lunch

& walked downtown with Berthe Arnold on one errand before supper, so it wasn't so bad.

I was most awfully glad to get your letter this afternoon. When a feller isn't feeling well he's apt to get lonesomer'n common, even if there are plenty of people around. I had a wire from Father too which I answered.

Thursday

Where do you think I am now? It's one o'clock & I'm sitting in a taxi outside the Senate office building, guarding banners. We rode down before twelve in Mrs. White's big car, loaded with banners. We drove in and while the car moved slowly around the circle, Moller, Jamison, Ainge[30] & Wold slipped out with their banners & made for the steps. Heavens! What activity around there for a few seconds!

Officers dashed from all sides, welcoming us with open arms & the four of them were immediately arrested & the car ordered off the grounds. I was the only one left in the car (with the chauffeur) & we drove outside the gates & stopped. I got out to come back & find Miss Paul & when I turned around, low & behold the car had driven off! I had to rush back to Headquarters, call a taxi, load in more banners & dash back again.

The rest were waiting opposite the Senate Office building, where a picket was immediately established, unmolested. I'm waiting to take my turn.

Time has elapsed.

I am now in the office of the Captain of Capitol Police. I did my turn on the steps of the Senate Office Building. And then Vivian Pierce & I got in the taxi, drove clear around the square & in another drive, descended upon an unprotected spot & got clear to the top of the center flight before officers could reach us. We refused to give up our banners & were dragged down here, our banners torn loose—we were told to go. We went back to Miss Paul at the S.O. [Senate Office] Bldg, each of us took a new banner & this time we walked with them straight up the center of the Avenue to the Capitol steps, where we were met & again escorted down here.

Our point is that they have no right to arrest us time after time, turning us loose each time & confiscating our property. So we refuse to give up our property without charges against us. This last time both of us got our wrists pretty badly wrenched. Clara Wold & Gladys Greiner were brought in next, pretty much banged up. A mob is collecting. Mrs. Moller & Mary Gertrude Fendall have come in now.

Later

This is the fourth time for me. The men have calmed down some by now. The first time or two they were so enraged they simply trembled with fury when they dragged us around. One officer was so beside himself that a man in the crowd urged him to be careful or he'd do something he'd be sorry for—and the man got brought along.

One officer scratched his hand on Mrs. Moller's banner and circulated the report that she had bitten him. People actually believe it.

Don't worry about me—I'm all right. They're probably keeping us just until Senate adjourns. I'll mail this as soon as I get out.

This has certainly been one exciting day for a person with Influenza!

Lots of love, Elizabeth

At the end of the letter, Elizabeth noted in pencil: "Home Again."

Saturday Morning, October 12, 1918

In this letter, Elizabeth mentions the "willful 34." Senator Albert Cummins, R-IA, had noted during debate: "I fear that a little group of willful men are intent on bringing about the defeat of this amendment." The NWP targeted these thirty-four Democrats and Republicans who voted no.

Everything peaceful today. Senate not in session at the Capitol, so we picketed in shifts of one hour each on the steps of the S.O. Bldg. I did my shift from 4 to 5 & then went down to the station and got a taxi to bring us home in.

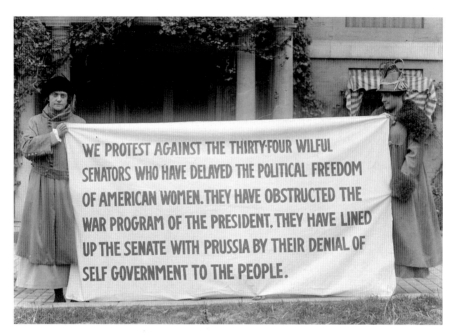

Bertha Moller and Berthe Arnold holding a banner targeting the thirty-four senators who were blocking passage of the suffrage act, 1918. *Library of Congress.*

You see and hear all kinds of things while you're picketing. One big red-faced individual said, "Huh! You think you're smart, don't you?!" for all the world like an angry little boy. Some just laugh. So many of the woman pass haughtily by with that charming, self-righteous expression on their faces, but many stop, interested.

One Senator stopped on the steps to assure us "*I* wasn't one of the 'willful 34'!" One said, "You're making a mistake, ladies, I voted for the amendment—but this is unpardonable." One stopped, read the banner then lifted his hat high and bowed beamingly. Another said, "Good work girls, keep it up!" Our dear friends Dodge and Reed pass by without seeing us at all.

Small boys taunt and yell. Bigger ones sneer. A few men stop and ask frankly for our point of view and some are impressed and some are not. One man stopped and asked me if they were really allowing us to stay there without protest. "I can hardly believe it," he said, "but they know they don't dare go too far."

I've got to get to work now, Love, Elizabeth

A Change of Position

Sunday Evening, October 13, 1918

Dearest Folks: Your dear letters, Father's of Tuesday & yours of Wednesday, came, cheering me up a lot. Though things have been happening so fast that I really couldn't be said to have been in need of cheering or comforting—no time for it!

I was so glad and relieved to know that Dr. Lindlahr thought I had handled my case successfully. Yes, I knew I had been pretty sick & that the fever had been pretty high. But I suppose I didn't realize just how seriously. Being out of my head, or half out, the biggest part of the time kept me from getting frightened or realizing, most likely. I used to "come to" & find myself sitting on or crawling up the big staircase at 2 or 3 o'clock at night, almost too weak to get up or down. And one night I was driven nearly frantic by the noises of work on the car tracks down Pennsylvania Ave, the rivetter & banging of steel rails & shouts of men & I went clear to the fourth floor to the hall window to find the noise & the flash of lights out in the Park blinded my weak eyes so that I sat down on the stairs & wept, fully convinced that my eyes had been put out. That was at 3:30 a.m. I don't know how I ever got up the stairs or down again.

You know my room has a window onto the alleyway between this house & the next at the side & the whole while I was sick they were delivering coal & shoveling it in, the incessant clash & bang of which tormented me nearly to death, and the automobiles chugging through the narrow resounding passage way, and the inevitable gasoline exhaust, which would fill my room and wake me up with the most oppressive feeling in my overburdened heart.

Julia Emory, in the next room, had some weird hallucinations, too. Her pet stunt was wandering about the house rescuing people from closets and once she announced to Miss Ainge, who had come in with her lunch, that she was perfectly stiff & couldn't move—all her inside had been cut out! Miss A. promised her that they would put them back & sew her up & she was satisfied then & relaxed.

I'm thankful to say that we have plenty of fuel now & have fires in the big grates, so we're comfortable & you needn't worry about the house being damp & cold.

Julia Emory pointing out her prison pin, given to suffragists who spent time in jail for picketing, circa 1917. *Library of Congress.*

My period only lasted the usual three days, though it was a week or more early. And tho the flow was very heavy, I was caused no pain or trouble. Last night I had a hot lemonade & a chest pack according to instructions & today the last lingering pain in my lungs was vanished. Yesterday my breathing had been rather difficult & quite painful.

I am being very careful not to overdo, to work steadily at any one thing, or to do much running around or climbing of stairs. And I spend a good deal of time out of doors, walking or sitting in the Park. Friday evening Jamie & Miss Wood & I went for a lovely carriage drive, got the carriage for only fifty cents a piece & rode for nearly two hours. It refreshed us wonderfully & was so restful & beautiful.[31]

Miss Wood, I find, studied under Herrick[32] years ago & we have much of interest to talk of together. She is a teacher and I like her immensely.

You'd like Jamie. She's different from anyone I ever knew, so independent & sensible & whimsical & droll—very decided in her likes & dislikes, very reticent & quiet usually. We seemed to "sort of" take to each other from the first & [I] was very much flattered at her interest in me because she had impressed me as so decidedly worthwhile. She is a good deal smaller than I am and is 28, with a face like a child's & she has bobbed hair. She was given a *7 months* prison sentence last year & served 2 months of it before she was released. She is Asst. Treasurer....

I am feeling a great deal stronger at the end of this week, though I still have sudden unaccountable spells of "giving out" and I realize, as everyone is trying to impress on me, that I must be careful and I am. So please don't worry.

There's no danger of my going to jail. The authorities have suddenly undergone an unexpected accession of common sense & realize that nothing could have helped the cause more than the prison sentences & now they declare that under no circumstances will they jail us and "allow us to pose as martyrs."

We had some perfectly beautiful publicity in all the New York & Philadelphia & Washington papers today and I hope you got to see it in the Chicago ones. Am sending you the bulletin that was released to the press, but you should have seen the write ups and comments we got! It is perfectly killing the way they so innocently play into Miss Paul's hands! I went out to the Hotels and bought all the New York and Phil papers for her today and then went through them & clipped & noted.

You see, we say: if we are not to be allowed to stand quietly *outside* the Senate & protest peacefully with our banners, then we'll go *inside* on the floor of the Senate & protest by words. Logical, isn't it?

Of course, tho' the poor bewildered things can't get our point of view, we never expect to get near the doors. But we are giving out our program in the most serene way and we *have* got them worrying, as there is evidence enough already, and we *will* give their police something to do and we *will* make evident the fact that our protests shall continue until something is done.

It's eleven o'clock and my wrist is giving out, for I've been addressing envelopes by hand for the better part of the day, along with several others (to the whole membership list, for which there are no addressograph plates—I had done the 4,500 on the Suffrage list, you know). But before I stop I must tell you the news.

Miss Paul has offered me the Suffragist Circulation Dept and asked me to stay & take it. I am to stay on as I am now until I get quite well & strong from the Flu, about another week will see me all right I think, but I'll be quite sure before I begin. And then I'm to take Miss Virginia Arnold's place, at $100 a month to start with and $125 later. I'm to move upstairs to a nice warm little room by myself, which will cost me $15 a month (outside roomers pay $30 a month & up, which is *cheap* for Washington). And I can either board in the Tea Room at $10 a week or take my meals out, but I have found that it is cheaper & food is better to eat here. Prices everywhere are terrific.

I told Miss Paul I would take it and she seemed pleased. What do you think about it, you folks? I think it may lead to other very valuable opportunities and it's work in which I'll be pretty much my own master & not under anyone. I will love the chance to try to build up the circulation, which is the most vital part of the whole work, Miss. P. thinks.

Talk to me about it. If for any reason either of you thinks it's not best, and I agree with you, I can always give it up. I'll like it very much better being here at Headquarters & in Washington & connected with the *Suffragist* than out organizing in these days of uncertain travel.

Vivian Pierce warned me against organizing. She said the Party doesn't pay enough to cover all expense & that one is continually having to dig down into one's own to help out, which is all right for a person who is independent of their salary, but which keeps anyone like her or myself continually pinching & scraping & paying back.

She and Mrs. Moller go to New Jersey to start campaigning tomorrow. Julia Emory goes soon, too, and Nita Pollitzer goes to her own state, South Carolina. I'm very fond of Julia Emory. She's a girl with a lot to her and as lively and funny as can be. She was nearly ruined by bad treatment & lack of necessities in prison during her period & now she has awful times—blood oozes out of the soles of her feet & her fingertips when she menstruates.

Nita Pollitzer I don't care as much for as some of the others. She's remarkably broad for a Southern girl born & bred, but there

Nita Pollitzer checking Tennessee legislature vote counts with W.J. Jameson, chair of the National Finance Committee of the Democratic Party, circa August 1920. *Library of Congress.*

really isn't much depth to her & to me she's very exasperating to do business with. She's one of the most successful money getters in the Party, though.

Berthe Arnold, from Color. Springs is going to be here this winter too, as the older Miss Arnold's Secretary in Executive work. I'm glad, for I like her. She stands beside me in the statue group of Lucy Branham & the torch. Lucy is going to Louisiana. She's a most successful organizer. Isn't she pretty? Berthe Arnold is too and to me seems somehow the spirit of the big, free lovely West.

Miss Paul will be gone in the States most of the time.

Jamie seemed awfully tickled when I told her my news this p.m. Just had my talk with A.P. today. I hope you all approve....

Heaps of love to you & my best to all who remember me, Elizabeth

Kicked and Detained

October 14, 1918
Capitol Guard Room

Here we are assembled again.

Miss Ainge was arrested for carrying the American flag. The police met our little single file band four abreast and dragged us and our banners apart. We proceeded to the Senate steps. The doors were barred by mobs of police and civilians. Most of us were arrested for nothing at all. The man that dragged me off was not even an officer.

We have tried to phone for a lawyer and they disconnected the phone. We tried to send a message to our Senators protesting against being arrested without cause, held without charges and allowed no redress. They refused to deliver the messages. Miss Paul (she is with us) demanded a lawyer or someone, saying they had no legal right to hold us without. They said oh yes, they could do whatever they liked, that we were merely being detained and didn't need a lawyer. Miss Paul then put her hand through the glass door and was thrown back into the room.

We have stormed the doors twice since and the men nearly go beside themselves with rage. Didn't you suppose that an officer of the *law* would be expected to discharge his duties in a calm and orderly manner and without losing his temper?

They kick and use their fists. They tremble with rage. They permit men to gather outside and jeer and peer in at us—which bothers us not at all, however.

It is now 5:30, and we are still held. Of course the Senate has adjourned long ago.

[Later:] They let us out at seven o'clock.

NWP protesters, including Elizabeth, begin unloading a carload of banners near the Senate Office Building, October 14, 1918. *Library of Congress.*

The women march down and around to the Senate entrance. Elizabeth is toward the back of the line, bracing herself for possible violence. October 14, 1918. *Library of Congress.*

Police grabbing banners from the suffragists. Elizabeth said: "Miss Ainge was arrested for carrying the American flag." She identified the women who were having their poles and banners grabbed by police as Bertha Moller and Elizabeth McShane. October 14, 1918. *Library of Congress.*

I have had a salad and a baked apple for my supper, and shortly I am going to bed with a hot lemonade inside me and a cold pack outside me. It was both cold and stuffy in the guard room today and I have something of a headache. I may rest in bed tomorrow.

Your letter that came this morning and the one from Miss Stevens which was waiting for me this evening make me homesick. I don't know whether I want to stay for the winter or not. What's the use of spending all our time away from each other?

Goodnight—I want a home of our own and I want to stay in it. Your homesick baby.

Tuesday Morning, October 15, 1918

I stayed in bed all morning and will spend the afternoon quietly out of doors. I'm not feeling worse, don't be worried. I'm just following your instructions and taking this opportunity to be quiet and rest up. Don't you think I'm wise and sensible?

The slight headache that I acquired yesterday is all gone, after a good night's sleep. Love, E.

Wednesday, October 16, 1918

I wish you didn't have to be so worried all the time about me. I have told you so many times (but it takes the mail so long to get there even when it isn't lost) that I *am* so much better, and that I *am* being careful, and they are not going to arrest us—that is, sentence us. They have stated as much. But of course, I can realize how you look at it and that you can't help worrying about what may possibly maybe perhaps happen anyhow—but you would do that whatever or whenever I was doing.

If you will just realize *this*, that I have come to realize myself more each day, that this has been more of an illness than the short duration of it at first led me to believe—because as each day goes by I still find myself nervous and fidgety and mentally very stupid and blurry, though my strength has largely come back and my heart and lungs are behaving properly. So that I am just as determined as you would have me to conserve my strength and get myself completely built up again. Just do believe that & you won't need to worry so much, because I *am* coming on beautifully.

It's just that sort of lassitude—more mental than physical—that bothers me now and makes it impossible for me to think clearly or write a logical letter or talk or even read or do any one thing long at a time without flying all to pieces. That, I realize, is due to the fact that my depleted energies are busy at other things—at building up, etc.—and haven't time to bother with my head. Therefore I shall be doubly sure to give them a chance.

So you think you ought to be entitled to wear a [military mother] service pin? Not many people would think so. In most eyes I am a traitor or a German and a few other things equally bad.

You ask, why we are trying to picket the Capitol "unlawfully." The explanation is this: Nobody knew anything about this little long-buried regulation until after we had attempted to picket the first time. At that time they did not arrest us or prefer any charge against us. They said, as they have said on every subsequent occasion, that they were merely "detaining" us.

Now Miss Paul argues that if we are not arrested and charged we are not breaking any law and that the women of the U.S. have a right to peacefully protest to their Senators at the doors of the Senate, in asking for simple justice at their hands. Where else can they go and to whom else? That they continue to deprive us of our property and our liberty, still insisting—with every insult thinkable—that we are not arrested and still refusing to allow us a lawyer is only calculated to make us more determined.

Wouldn't it be to you?

Of course Red Cross and Liberty Loan banners are and have been carried onto the Capitol grounds. What is there more harmful in a Suffrage tricolor than in either of those? We have not since attempted to display a lettered banner.

The fact that we have even been arrested for carrying the American flag or for attempting to enter the lower public door of the Senate building (recognized because we wore suffrage sashes under our coats) is enough to show the motive behind it all.

Of course, as you know by this time from an earlier letter, the story carried (with variations, I suppose) by the Sunday papers was solely for the purpose of gaining publicity for the fact that we had so far been denied the right to stand peaceably outside.

I suppose though that afterwards [they] carried all sorts of lies and wrong impressions of Monday's happenings, in line with the usual stuff, like biting policemen or like that editorial from the *Tribune*. I showed that to a man who stopped at the Tea Room cash box last evening to ask what sort of publicity we had gotten and he was greatly edified. "Well, as long as you know and everybody knows if they're honest, that the issue is liver than it's ever been, you can afford to ignore that kind of junk," he said.

And I agree, though it does make you furious that people can't know the truth.

Personally I think as Vivian Pierce does, that we have gone far enough with the Capitol attempts and should confine our picketing to the S.O. Bldg steps, that we'll gain nothing more now in keeping up the other. But I think that Miss Paul intends to continue the other [picketing at the Capitol] whenever the Senate is in session—for a while at least. But you see, we're really annoying

NWP protestors in front of the Senate building, before detention: Mildred Gilbert of California, Pauline Floyd of D.C. and Vivian Pierce of California. 1918. *Library of Congress.*

no one but the police now, it seems to me, and there's no special point in doing that.

I'm anxious to hear from you in answer to my Sunday evening letter and see what you think of my new proposition. I'm going to move into a nice room upstairs in the morning....

Miss Stevens told me in her letter about your seeing "Polly" together and I'm so glad you did. The theatres are all closed here as are schools, churches, etc.[33]

It's getting late so I think I must hie me to bed, as I must be up betimes in the morning. I'll got out & mail this now. With all my love & hoping you won't need to be so alarmed again, Elizabeth

Tuesday, October 17, 1918

I've just come back from the Capitol and am sitting out in the Park to write. I did two hours on the picket line today—yesterday and today have been gloriously warm, sunny days, and I've enjoyed being out on picket in the sun. I feel like a new person. The Senate was in session for only a half hour today, so there was "nothing doing" there.

The plan had been to exhibit the first of the special "Willful 34" banners today had the session lasted, but now that will have to wait until Monday. As Senator Sheppard said to us today on the steps, "meeting two days a week, short sessions, for lack of 'pressing' business. Don't you think we might get down to something *really important?*" Senator Sheppard is a dandy, all right.

Today's banner was to have been for Wadsworth (R-NY) and said that he would do well to rejoin his regiment and fight for liberty abroad instead of staying here and fighting against democracy at home.[34]

Each of the 34 will be taken up in turn. They will be displayed by one person alone and in this way they can be gotten up on the steps and held for at least a moment before being removed, which will be sufficient for the newspapers. Edith Ainge of New York will carry the New York banner.

The populace and the police both looked rather disappointed that we stayed peacefully on the Senate Office steps today. Both had assembled up in front of the Capitol in large numbers. As one Senator said today: "Isn't it peculiar—you stand here with your banners and you are peaceful citizens; you cross that little square with them and you immediately become bold, bad, terrible women!"

Senator Smoot (this ink in my pen is so terrible, I'll have to resort to a pencil) said when he passed us yesterday: "Well, girls, does your Mother know you're out?"

Nearly everybody comments that we "look like a bunch of schoolgirls," in a surprised manner as though they expected us to be old & withered & disappointed in love. It's funny.

I spent the better part of this morning getting moved upstairs. I'm very comfortably and cheerfully located now, with two airy windows out high above neighboring roofs, and a cot and desk and table and dressing table and plenty of drawers and hooks for my clothes—and I'm right next door to a bathroom. Also I have a big radiator.

You should have seen me today, arrayed in the latest Washington fashion, white pumps, black stockings, white dress, black hat.

That's it. And it was most convenient that it should have been the latest thing in smartness, for I wanted to wear my white suit and I had no clean mended white socks. To have been entirely in the swim I lacked only a "Gas Mask" for influenza, "everyone is wearing them." Do they appear in correct Chicago circles?

As you may see by the papers, the situation is terribly serious here. Death rate was 90 for yesterday and new cases still on the increase. It is worst, of course, among the newly arrived government workers, who are mostly living in crowded conditions and who are self-dependent and have no one to care for them. All the employees of the various bureaus have "recesses" morning and afternoon when they are required to go out in the parks for air.

I began yesterday to take a little instruction in the workings of my new department, and if I keep on feeling better each day I think likely I'll start in in earnest on Monday. A.P. warned me not to start too soon and I shall not. They'll probably still need me for part time picketing each day, for which I am glad for its great fun. It's a joy to be with Julia Emory in any sort of enterprise. She's so full of vim and enthusiasm and so utterly fearless of public censure, afraid of nothing in the world if she thinks she's right. We have picketed together each time, she has charge of recruiting the picket line.

The past few days we've been so bold as to take our banners back and forth on the streetcar, and as they are rather large and conspicuous affairs it has taken quite skillful management and has been great fun shocking the public. The conductors are all our friends and say "all aboard for the Suffrage special" and similar things when the car stops for passengers.

Of course you can't imagine me doing the things I'm doing, nobody could. Because the me that is doing them is one that has only just been born. I don't think the new me has affected the old one in any way and probably when this phase of my work is over with it will get back to sleep again until needed.

You ask me how I feel about it all. Well, really, it is like looking on the performances of a perfectly detached personality most of the time. I never feel self-conscious of the stares and jeers of the mob when I'm in a conspicuous position. I'm able to go through it all quite quietly and undisturbedly, because I know that I'm just one of many, and because I am unknown, and because I know that I am right and the others merely do not understand.

There's never yet been a reform movement that was not misunderstood—until after it succeeded. George Washington would today be an ignominious traitor if the revolution had failed. The revolutionary colonists were at first a wicked minority among a Tory majority. And so it goes.

I couldn't do these things—I couldn't even interview Senators—if I wasn't upheld by the spirit and the courage of all these other girls and women. It is their spirit which enters into one and holds me up. Also I will admit that it would be much harder in a community where I was well and widely known, like Houston....[35]

Suppertime now, so I'll send this off for today. With heaps of love, your very busy & happy Daughter

October 19, 1918

Dear Mother: I had a letter from Father today telling me of Grandmama's improved condition and I have written to him direct to allay his fears about me. So you needn't send this note on.

Of my condition, I have as I told him practically regained my strength apparently but am continuing to be most careful. Did not even picket today as it was pretty cold. Did envelopes nearly all day instead, except for a nice brisk walk in the afternoon. Sat by a lovely blazing big, open fire. And as to my heart & lungs, all trouble seems over there, though I am again continuing my cautious attitude. And I am most of all thankful to state that my brain has come out of its semi-retired state & is again condescending to be more active.

Do understand this, that at no time did I intentionally keep you ignorant of or under a misapprehension concerning my condition. I simply didn't realize myself at that time and I thought when the lapse of the fever left me in such great relief that I was well—as after any ordinary cold.

Today I am enjoying some nice sore muscles after resumption (very gradually, however) of my morning & evening exercises yesterday. Of course I only do a few very easy and non-exhausting ones yet—but had not been able to do *any* before that, on account of pounding effect on my heart. Even bending made me blindly dizzy....

I was so glad to have your nice letter of Wednesday and know you approved of my plan. I am getting more and more enthusiastic all the time. Miss Fendall (the treasurer) was thoughtful enough today to suggest that she advance me half a month's salary, knowing that I had been here a good while [over a month] without earning anything. So I have received my first N.W.P. check for $50.00 and will deposit it at "our" bank on Monday. I still had almost $20.00 of what I brought with me, however. But it was nice of her to think of it.

I'm rather like Jamie. She came to Washington to Headquarters two years ago, after giving up her job...with no assurance of one here, and with $25.00 in her pocket....

I'll be most glad of any list of possible subscribers you can send for me to write to after I get "in" and am glad of suggestions made....I will have to write all my own soliciting letters and do it gradually, for the daily routine is quite time-absorbing in itself. I am so tremendously glad of everyone's interest.

My name is already up on my office door—"Miss Kalb—Business Department—Suffragist" and I swell up visibly as I pass it. Quite a bit better than a place in an ad office at $12 per week, isn't it? Our waitresses get $12.50, without any perceptible College education! Am very gratified and pleased over Dr. L's interest in the work and methods of the Party....

The first time he [policeman] was very nice and fatherly and said "Well little girl, I am with you for Suffrage but you're hurting your cause this way." And I smiled and hung on to the banner and I followed him to the guard room. The second time he grinned at me and said, "Well you rascal, here you are again!" And I said nothing. And the third and fourth times I fell to the lot of other and more vicious ones. And the next time he got me he had become perceptibly exasperated, in fact he quite shook with—er—exasperation. And he said nothing until we reached the guard room, when he endeavored to remove the banner, and he remarked rather heatedly, "Let go that banner or by God I'll make you!" And I replied, "I will not, I'll keep it myself. You have no right to steal my property unless I'm charged with some offence." Whereupon he answered by bending back my thumb and twisting my wrist and jerking the pole away with a pull that sent me spinning. At all subsequent times his remarks were too sputtery and disjointed to reassemble here....

I had the cashbox tonight and must now go do the half hour more I promised Nita and her envelopes. Love, E.

Picket Lines and Envelopes

Sunday, October 20, 1918

Dearest Ones,

...The large [photograph] enclosed for you now was taken of tail end of line at Capitol Monday.

As you will see, I (third from end) have not yet been molested. We had just marched into grounds from Senate Office Bldg (in background). The mob is all up ahead, out of the picture. The first one with policeman is Mrs. Moller. The other battling one is Elizabeth McShane....

Picketed for an hour & half this p.m. We displayed the Wadsworth[36] banner at our old stand instead of waiting for Monday at the Capitol. Maybe it didn't create some excitement! People seemed to enjoy it hugely. He's not liked, you know. He has such a consistently reactionary record.

I must stop now and go down and do envelopes. You would die laughing at Nita Pollitzer (who has charge of the envelopes).

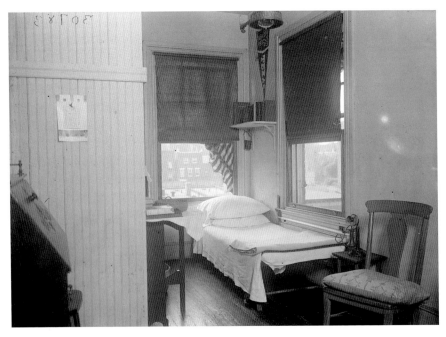

Elizabeth's bedroom at NWP headquarters. Note the Texas pennant hanging above the bookcase and two windows giving her plenty of light and air. August 1919. *Library of Congress.*

She goes out in the Park and corrals perfectly harmless humans to come in and address envelopes. And no one can enter headquarters without her nabbing them. The way she does it is most refreshing. Most people would be appalled at the prospect of 50,000 envelopes to address. But not she.

I'm quite fascinated with my new little room & slept fine in it last night.

Two nights ago, when I resumed my sitz [bath], was the first night since beginning of illness that I slept really *soundly*. Certainly noticed the difference. Now that am in my own room can begin my window airbaths again. How I've missed the *real* airbath![37]

Heaps of love, Elizabeth

[P.S.] Have you seen any copies of the enclosed *War Weekly*, edited by George Harvey[38] of the *North American Review*?...It is a marvel that its publication is permitted these days. How it has escaped I can't see. Master of high-handed sarcasm certainly. Read everything in it, don't miss a thing!

ELIZABETH'S MOTHER, BENIGNA KALB, apparently contacted Alice Paul directly to express concern for her daughter's condition and request she not be used in picketing. An outgoing, supremely confident woman, Benigna never hesitated in going directly to the top official. And while she may not have caused "extra trouble" for Elizabeth, the twenty-one-year-old may not have appreciated the interference.

Monday Evening, October 21, 1918

Dear Mother Mine: Your letter of Friday evening came to me today, with Father's of Wednesday enclosed. My dear, you certainly don't think you need to *apologize* for being interested enough to worry about me, do you? I certainly don't wonder that you *did* worry, under the circumstances. And it certainly did *not* cause me extra trouble on account of it. I was only cross to think that because of lost or delayed letters you had been made to worry unnecessarily.

I'm sorry that yesterday before your request came to me [to not picket] I had already promised Julia Emory faithfully that I would go in the Capitol line today, and she is having such a desperate time these days to keep her lines going, with so many people sick and out of the city that I didn't have the heart to desert her. As it turned out, I was really glad to spend two hours in a warm room at the Capitol rather than to have picketed even an hour up on the Senate steps, for though it was bright and sunny today, and not cold, the wind was frightfully strong and quite sharp.

Also everything was quite calm and peaceful. A group of four picketed the S.O. steps as usual, with the new [Senator] Shields banner, while four of us attempted to picket in a similar manner the Capitol steps with the Wadsworth banner and tricolors.

Then a second squad was to have followed us shortly, with the Shields banner, while the "stationary pickets" were to have held the original "34 willful men" banner in their accustomed place. But some boys kidnapped the last named banner as it lay folded up on the steps, and ran off with it, so we couldn't risk the Shields banner, and only one deputation could be sent to the Capitol. But as it turned out, the Senate adjourned very soon, so it didn't matter.

We four were stopped in the middle of the plaza as usual, but this time we had decided not to resist unduly their taking the banners from us, just to test whether in that event we would be left free to go our way—so there was no violence. But though the police insisted on taking the banners from us they nevertheless secured us firmly by the arm and marched us quietly but emphatically down the terrace and into the building for the customary detention.

We were put in a different and quite bare room this time and the glass in the doors was perforated tin. But the room was warm and well-ventilated and the chairs comfortable and Miss Arnold (Miss Virginia Arnold, it is, the one I'm "learning my trade" from) read us a story of Upton Sinclair's from a little paper she had in her pocket. We four were Julia Emory, Matilda Young (sister of Joy Young, the organizer), Miss Virginia Arnold and Myself.

We were unmolested and at 2:30, when the Senate adjourned, were released and came home.

Anita Pollitzer leaves tonight for Wyoming, to organize.[39] Miss Paul and Miss Younger expect to leave soon for the East.

I am spending a good part of each day in the office with Virginia Arnold, learning the routine....Would you do me a little bundle and send me? My old plaid skirt will be of service...and my knitting bag will come in handy for all kinds of excursions....

Good night and all my love, Elizabeth

Virginia Arnold with the Kaiser Wilson banner that sparked an angry crowd response. Some believed this was sedition. August 1917. *Library of Congress.*

On October 22, a New York newspaper carried the story of Elizabeth's arrest. The paper also reported a "near riot" as office boys attacked the women.[40]

Wednesday, October 23, 1918

Dearest Mumsey: After working on envelopes *all* day yesterday and until rather late at night, my hand and brain both refused to write you a letter last night when I got upstairs. Now that Anita has gone to Wyoming, Miss Paul has turned that job over to me. There won't be more than another day of addressing, I hope—then comes stamping and folding of letters.

What do you think next? Miss Paul had a wire last night from the organizer who has been working in his state that at an interview with Pollock (D-SC) he had *pledged his vote*! Another one! We're almost safe now, *providing* the Democrats do not yet in some way prevent its coming up again. Hence the continuance of picketing and demonstrations until the thing is actually done....

The NWP switchboard that Elizabeth learned to use. Summer of 1919. *Library of Congress.*

I am feeling fine these days. Yesterday was ideal. Picketed from 4 to 5.

Later. I have been summoned to tend the switchboard for an hour as our operator did not appear. Very exciting work when the calls come quick and fast! Soon I must get ready to go out for my picket duty.

Later. A small mob tore up today's banner before our squad arrived on the scene. It was termed "seditious." Will send you tomorrow the press notices about it. Julia and Jamie, without banner and only wearing sash colors, attempted to cross street into Capitol grounds to protest to police and were put out bodily by squad of police and plainclothes men. I very dutifully kept out of it.

Will write a real letter tomorrow. Lots of Love, E.

Friday, October 25, 1918

Dearest Folks: Your letters have been coming & coming & I haven't really answered one properly for some time. I have been working so steadily at envelopes, with just time off in the afternoons for picketing, that I just couldn't write any more. I ran off last evening tho' right after supper with Jamie, and left my poor volunteers writing away alone in the ballroom. We crept out the little dark postern gate into the alley like two conspirators from on ancient castle and fled. I felt as though I could *not* have sat still any longer.

So we walked and walked and walked, down F St. to look at the shops and over past the beautiful Public Carnegie Library, which I had not seen, and out Massachusetts Ave—then back to sit in the park opposite Headquarters for a while to watch the people stroll by. When we came in I was so sleepy from the fresh air and the exercise that I just tumbled into bed.

All afternoon I had been trying a new stunt. I sat perfectly still from 2 o'clock until 6:30 in a taxi drawn up by the curb of the Senate office building, guarding ten tricolors and waiting for Julia Emory and V. Arnold to be released. A very different matter, sitting there on the same level, from standing up on the steps with a banner. Imagine being perfectly oblivious to scornful glances, disrespectful grins and virtuous indignation—as well as the shouts of small boys—for four hours and a half.

My chauffeur finally took pity on me and very gallantly bought me a *Saturday Evening Post* to read. He was a very decent and respectful taxi driver—just a kid, with a very dirty face. He was very indignant at the police and chased all the boys who tried to snatch the banners. It was really very funny. Because if he had not happened to feel that he was "in the game," he'd probably have been as ready as the rest to jeer at us.

There was no picketing on the S.O. steps. A.P. has stopped that and is trying to force the issue at the Capitol before recess on the 29th. What then, I don't know. But yesterday the plan was for the same two to keep going back as fast as they were released. We didn't know, in view of the happenings of the day before, how long they'd be kept. Whether just until Senate adjourned or longer, or how long the Senate would be in session. They *had* been adjourning each time at 2:30.

The two girls, Miss Paul & I drove down (up, I should say) about 1:30, deposited the three of them about a block in front of the Capitol & then I drove around the Capitol grounds and up at the side of the S.O. Bldg in the accustomed place, the reserve banners flaunting out the back of the car. I was to wait there until Miss Paul came back to report and give further instructions. And in event of certain contingencies I was to do certain other things.

In the meantime the two [Julia Emory and Virginia Arnold], with an oilcloth banner rolled up and carried inconspicuously between them and with Miss Paul trailing some distance in the rear to observe things, came peacefully up the front approach. A crowd was gathered at the foot of the Senate steps gazing at a captured cannon, relic of the Marne, which was on exhibition there. The top of the flight was empty save for one lone guard. (I neglected to mention that the Capitol Police were drawn up 15 strong at the other entrance, watching me and my banners across the street.)

The girls stopped and inspected the gun, continued on their way, stopping half way up the steps to sit down and rest a minute, climbed on, and when they reached the top, suddenly whipped out the banner and stood with it there between them for several whole minutes before the guard could realize what had happened. And there was the crowd, all ready to observe and read the banner.

The guard finally took in the situation and grabbed Julia, but he couldn't manage them both and there they still stood with the banner stretched wide while he yelled down the steps—"Policeman! Come get this woman!"—and until the policeman could climb the steps. If they could only have known how relieved the girls were at being taken immediately, for they had dreaded a repetition of the mob of Monday—it was a duplicate of the so-called "German" banner they were carrying.

But they were removed to the guard room and locked up and treated very gently. You see they weren't the regular Capitol Police that handled them this time, they hadn't got used to handling women roughly.

The evening before Julia and Jamie had been jerked and pulled and pounded, until they were sore and bruised all over. Jamie was given such a jerk by the sash over her shoulder that the wide heavy satin ribbon was split right off her. You can imagine where such a violent pull landed *her*. Also they were "damned" and otherwise appellated by a plainclothes man among them.

But this time there was no roughness, due to the inexperience of the guards. The regulars were thereupon dispersed about the grounds, however, to watch for another such surprise, leaving only four to watch me and the taxi. Before that, though, one would semi-occasionally detach himself from the row and stroll casually across the street and past the cab to see if he could see anything brewing. It was all so comical that I could scarcely maintain my gravity.

Finally Miss P. came back, told me all the happenings, instructed me to wait till the girls came out and then went home.

The Senate did not adjourn until 4:30 and the girls were kept until 6:30, until the Capt. thot it too late for them to do anything more. It had clouded up during the p.m., so it was almost dark by then.

Several people came up at different times to talk about it, some I knew and some I didn't, and my taxi driver several times volunteered some tales about life as a taxi man to regale me, so the time was not so very terribly long as I could watch the people go by.

This boy [driver] had been working to and from the war-workers' emergency hospital and had seen 345 influenzas deaths removed from there. That's war-workers alone. He also discussed the relative merits of "waiting jobs" and "hauling jobs" and the relative dangers of wet streets, ice, and snow. He told about carrying an officer with a 44mm shell at a rapid pace to his destination and how he turned green with fright at the end of the trip when he learned that the shell had been in there; and of driving a drunken Congressman home; and other interesting facts.

Well, I have already related the rest of the evening's doings. But you see I have not been in any mobs and they are respecting your wishes as to keeping me out of the Capitol arrests for the present....

I'll be so glad when these envelopes are finished and I can get started at my own job. Almost all done now but stamping & folding of letters. 50,000. Whoop!

Well, this note has grown to quite decent proportions and I *must* stop now. Am feeling fine. With all my love. Elizabeth

BROKEN PROMISES

Elizabeth wrote the following on torn brown paper, with a linen tag marked "Senate" pinned to the top:[41]

Friday Afternoon, October 25, 1918
Guard Room

No'm, I have not busted my promise. The police busted it. In this wise:

Julia, Matilda Young and I came down the first hour today to peaceably picket the Senate Office steps, as usual.

They took the top of the steps with one of the big gold and white "We Demand an Amendment–" banners and I stood at the bottom in the center with a tricolor floating bravely in the wind.

Thus we stood for perhaps five minutes.

Then in the offing appeared Colonel Higgins, handsome Sergeant at Arms of the Senate, and at his heels 2 police. The police stayed on the curb across the street and the Colonel came

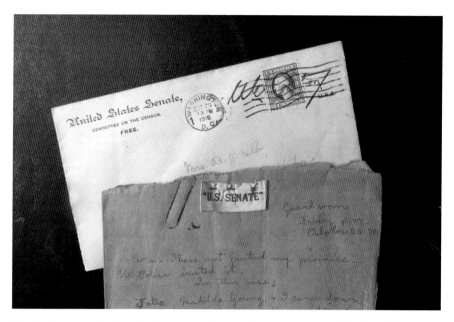

Elizabeth's souvenirs from the Senate guard room: brown paper shared by the suffragists, Senate ID tag and U.S. Senate envelope. October 25, 1918. *Handy/Marshall Collection.*

on. He passed me, ascended the steps and spoke to Julia. I could not tell what was happening, until I saw the 2 police come across the street and also ascend the steps. Then three dirty, ugly-looking plainclothes men who had been hanging about unnoticed, descended upon me.

I was so astonished I didn't know what to do. While one wrenched my banner away, two others grabbed me, one on each side. I was so furious I was afraid I would weep for rage. The nasty, dirty things!

Our policy is not to speak to the officers, but that got the best of me—one creature with both paws on one arm and another grabbing my other wrist, me wholly unresisting—so I said in a furious voice: "Does it take *both* you brutes to hold me?" So one of them let go my arm. And the other stood there and *deliberately* twisted my wrist as far 'round as he could! Just deliberately, with me not even *offering* to pull away! "Let go my wrist!" I demanded, which he finally did, grabbing my sleeve, and jerking me zip-zag all the way over to the Capitol, giving me here a pull and there a jerk so that I could not even walk straight. Imagine such treatment, even with the most hardened criminals who were not trying to escape.[42] My arm aches from fingers to shoulders from that twisting.

We are now here in the guard room. Jamie and Berthe Arnold, who came all unsuspectingly at 3 o'clock to relieve us on picket duty, have joined us here having been arrested also. We have no phone connection—as usual. This is all the paper we can find to write on. The men tried to scare us by talking about the rats in this room, as they brought us over.

I have just had a good compliment. Julia said to Matilda Young: "Gee—I never saw anyone with more spirit than Kalb for a new one!" So often, they say, perfectly courageous women get cold feet after they get here & back down or else it takes so long for them really to get into the spirit of thing. Coming from J. Emory, I certainly treasure that remark. "You'd be perfectly corking in jail," she said. "We'd never have to worry about you losing your nerve." They've spent the afternoon telling me all sorts of their prison experiences.

It's beginning to get dark and I suppose they'll release us soon.

It's perfectly great the way they've stupidly played into our hands & brazenly removed us from the S.O. steps after allowing us to say there peaceably since October 1. When it comes down to a matter of right, of course the Capitol Police had no right to molest us *off* the Capitol grounds. We were under District police jurisdiction there. But we hear it rumored that they were acting under orders of the *Dept of Justice!*

We divided our paper up evenly among us, so I'll have to stop as I've come to the end of mine. Will add a note & mail when we get out.

The next is written on a small piece of yellow paper, apparently mailed together with the above. The envelope Elizabeth used was a Senate one that she carried away with her from the Guard Room.

Headquarters

They let us out at 10:30 pm and we have just got home. Miss Paul has had everybody in the District telephoning the Capitol & the newspapers, protesting & asking for news. Everybody was tremendously excited. If they'd only kept us all night *what* a story that would have made! We had bolted ourselves in and made beds of chairs turned upside down and arranged to be quite comfortable.

The place was a sort of junkpile for all kinds of things & we found a sewing machine all threaded up & some sort of striped linen stuff for chair covers. Julia and I each made a lovely big laundry bag, with one of these U.S. Senate tags sewed on them, for souvenirs.

I am quite safe and none the worse for wear, except for a blister on one finger. I think I'll say the policeman bit it! Goodnight, E.

Sunday, October 27, 1918

Dear Mother: I didn't get to bed until after one last night and then I was too tired out and too sick (not physically) to write even a line on a postcard.

Yes, we were in all day again yesterday and we were very roughly handled in the taking, so that I am quite sore all over. But that is not why I felt as I did. I was just sick of the world and of humanity at large.

Last night about 8 o'clock (we had been released at 7) eight of us went back to the Senate Building steps with our tricolors.

And the police that descended upon us were drunk, and one of them struck our little Jamie and threw her so that she fell like a log on the marble paving, striking her head, and she lay there stunned and motionless.

Never have I felt such a terribly sickened drop of my spirits as when I saw her go down. None of us expected to find her alive when we reached her, for her head struck. But she was only stunned and badly bruised, though I didn't know until I got her home that she might not be hurt internally. I held her against me in the taxi, and her head was so limp on my shoulder. Never have I felt so wild with fury as alone with her in that cab last night, speeding home.

She seems all right again this morning, barring aches and bumps. But that does not take away one jot from the fact that a crowd of human creatures could stand all about us and watch 8 girls mauled and thrown and *kicked* by a force of drunken, irresponsible brutes of police. And that one of them could drag two of us out into the street and threaten to put us under the cars. And a *woman* come up to him and say, "Of course, Officer, you know I am *with you*, but be careful and don't go too far with the creatures, because you know that the more you hurt them the more they like it, posing as martyrs."

That a *woman* could say, "They're a disgrace to their sex— cheap notoriety hunters—no true suffragists"—and the drunken policeman answering—"Yes'm, I know they are!" And that woman was Mrs. Bass,[43] woman member from N.Y. of the Dem. Exec. Comm. To me she was ten times more contemptible than that poor brute that was hauling us about.

I was not hurt. I should have said that earlier. But I had Jamie with me, after we had got her up and she could walk again, and the man dragged us out through the crowd and onto the street instead of arresting us with the others, because, I think, he was afraid to do anything more to Jamie. So when I started back to find the others and found that the police were already proceeding with them across the Capitol plaza, I decided that the only thing to do was to get Jamie out of it as quickly as possible.

I was starting for a streetcar when the taxi driver who had brought us up rushed up to me and said he had the cab ready. He helped me put Jamie in, and then all the way home as I held her I simply wept with fury to think they had dared to do what they did. You cannot imagine what a sickening rage it inspires in one to stand helpless and watch a comrade hurt. As Julia says, it's much, much harder than getting hurt yourself. I think I could have killed that policeman.

That's the hard part. We dare not make the least move to resist or to fight back. They can make up lies about what we do fast enough without that.

Julia was tripped up and kicked and dragged up by her hair. I found out later, when the girls got home about twelve. To me everything was hazy and unreal like a horrible dream after I saw Jamie fall in that awful dead way and lie so still. I have just the vaguest impression of the crowd, and the lights, and the sound of struggle, and the swearing of policemen, and finally of being twisted and bent over my banner pole, dragged down the steps and shoved down into the street along with Jamie. I think that the fact of my sticking by Jamie is probably what saved me from rougher handling. As it was, I only got a crack over the head with a heavy banner pole, which left a nice lump and a headache and my right arm is rather stiff as a result of the twisting, also the small of my back.

But oh what a fury of indignation it all leaves in me! And a determination to do my part to show them that we are invincible.

The Senate recesses Monday until after elections, so we will have a respite. Some toughs in the crowd yelled "Atta boy! Go to it! Treat 'em rough!" But that Bass creature—fat, waddling slimy toad—made me angrier than anyone else. Some men, I am glad to say—army officers—tried to stop the police and the police promptly turned on *them*.

They never got my banner, tho', the tricolor part. I found myself still hanging onto it in the cab. And that tricolor I have kept *for myself*.

To think of even the commonest criminals being treated like we were. I hated to tell you all this but was afraid the papers might have it and you would be frightened not to hear. With my love, Elizabeth

Monday Morning, October 28, 1918

The enclosed letter, written yesterday, got mislaid downstairs among the envelopes. I didn't find it until now, so I'll add a little note before I send it off.

Yesterday we had one long afternoon & evening of sheer loveliness to heal the wounded spirits. Miss Ainge took Jamie & me out into the Country, to Rock Creek Park and through the beautiful, beautiful woods and hills and valleys all flaming with yellows and reds. An unending delight to the eye and we saw the bears, wolves, lions and tigers that inhabit the woody recesses of the [Zoo] park. (The park is entirely wild, unspoiled by a landscape gardener's conventionalizing hand.)

And then farther out into the country to Chevy Chase where at Brooke Farm lives Mrs. Brooke[44] of the Party [NWP], a very sweet, motherly sort of person. And there was such an exquisite atmosphere of peace over the whole out of doors and only the dear old colonial house which is more than 100 years old. And the charming, homey rooms, furnished with such lovely taste in old blues & white & dull creamy yellow & heirloom furniture.

And we were made to stay to the family Sunday night supper. And there was *real* milk and homemade butter & fluffy hot rolls like we used to make, with preserves and lettuce and sliced tomatoes and baked apples with cream.

And there was an old dear of a big shaggy shepherd dog.

And then there was the trip home through the delightful, invigorating air, under the stars & the open sky, and through the sweet, spicy fall smells of the country.

And then, wonderfully refreshed, we took our aching bones to bed.

I am reveling in being able to sleep once more without a nightgown now that I am alone. How my feet do long for a skip through the dewy grass, and what a joy an air bath and a real spray would be! And a real Elmhurst meal—! The food is remarkably good here and offers a splendid selection for me. But still, *of course*, the vegetables are not cooked as they are with you, good as they are.

I am not nearly so stiff this morning. Even at its worst, I was not one half as sore & stiff & bruised & bumped as I have been many times after a basketball game or after a long horseback ride or a paddling trip or a day in the garden. It's just the way you get it that makes it seem worse.

I had a letter from Lela just Saturday....She told me that Otto Cain & Ira South had died with the Flu in camp and also Will Nathan's sister.

I must stop now and get to stamping envelopes. With all my love, Elizabeth

War News and Picketing

Monday Night, October 28, 1918

Just a note to let you know that, tho' I think the papers are going to carry today's demonstration, it was the mildest (generally speaking) we have had yet, as far as treatment goes. With the exception of two men, nobody made any trouble. I was actually dazed at drawing such a lamb. He merely lowered my banner, allowed me still to hold it, took me very gently by the sleeve and marched me to the guard room. He said a few nasty things, but then stuff like that you can be oblivious to.

I was *so* thankful that we escaped a mauling that I could have wept on his shoulder. If they only knew how mild we really are! After you are actually into the struggle you don't mind it so much, because activity brings confidence & the brutes inspire you with contempt and determination not to give up. You'd even like to be permitted to give them a few wallops in return. It's the half hour or so beforehand that is the worst. Or the last few minutes when you see them coming for you. So it was a wonderful relief to be taken so peaceably.

But, as I said, not *all* of us were so fortunate. I had managed to elude policemen (who were busy, you may believe) and march straight on ahead of the whole line that had been stopped, before I was taken, so I was right up front and saw the two rough-handlings.

Miss Paul drew that awful plain-clothesman I told you about. And he pinned her arms and twisted them behind her and then put her other arm around her shoulders from behind and pushed her all the way, to make it appear that she was resisting. She had to bite her lips to keep from screaming. That drew a lot of indignation from the crowd—but nobody had enough spunk to interfere.

Then at the entrance steps—unfortunately around where the crowd couldn't see it—the same beast that knocked Jamie down the other night was jerking and pushing Mrs. Arniel toward the steps so violently that she tried to hold back to keep from falling. With that he threw her against the steps & her head struck & was badly cut just above the eye & her back so badly wrenched that she couldn't walk. He dragged her up when she screamed out at the pain and said savagely—"Here, get up, you ain't hurt—and if you are you did it yourself!" And literally dragged her by one arm through the door and into the guard room.

We did what we could for her with cold water and when the Captain of Police came in he was decidedly frightened. And they brought a stretcher and had her removed to the hospital. Tonight two of the girls went to see her after supper and found her a little hazy, but well cared for. But *this is what they* [the police] *told the nurses:*—that she had been hit by a streetcar! The nurses were simply incensed when they heard the truth. Her being carried out on a stretcher created a lot of comment.

We were only held until six, all twenty-four of us in that stuffy guard room. But it *was* a corking demonstration—24 springing up where eight had been beaten before. Lucy Burns was here and other women who had been to jail. And a Mrs. Lloyd from Chicago, who had met you at tea not long before. You must see her when she gets back.

I'm simply *dead* tired tonight. Why, I don't know, unless from the suspense and excitement beforehand, so I'll say goodnight. Yours, Elizabeth

Thursday, October 31, 1918
Elizabeth's Twenty-Second Birthday

My darlings—I have been sitting here & staring at the paper hard and thinking but not writing. It seems as though I can't get started at writing this, my birthday letter....How rich I am and shall always be in such a wonderful love as yours! I think when I see about me so many selfish, domineering fathers who don't know what it means to be tender, and so many careless, petulant mothers who either hinder or do not care or never try to understand—how blessed, truly blessed, am I in my parents! I cannot imagine what it would be to have been born as the big majority are born! People don't seem even to *expect* much tenderness and understanding in a father—and so often the idealized mother is very little more so. I tell you, it is not *motherhood* that is sacred; it is the *mother behind the motherhood*.

Tuesday, November 5, 1918

The following is an excerpt from Elizabeth's original letter, now lost.

Dear Mother: I started last night to answer the many questions which came in yesterday's letter, but I felt too weary from the day's fray to undertake it and I had thought so hard and incessantly that my mind was groggy...

It is not a physical weariness that gets you (yesterday I myself was not nearly so roughly handled as I have been many times before)—it's nerve-weariness and spirit-weariness. And the feeling of perfectly *impotent* fury—fury at our own helplessness to deal with such brutes—is the most exhausting emotion there is when it gets you into its grip.

Yesterday I know I could have done physical violence with the utmost joy to [badge] #21. The beast had his innings with Julia yesterday. We thought he had broken her wrists. Even she screamed—and when you get a cry or even a look of pain out of plucky Julia Emory, you can know that something has happened. But all anyone did was to jeer at her and laugh and imitate her: "Stop! Stop! You are breaking my wrists!" All this happened when we were beyond the view of the crowd, but under the eyes of Captain of Police himself.

Poor Julia was so faint and sick from the pain that she almost leaned on her guard as he walked her away. I tried to break away and go to her and got my own thumbs bent back and wrists twisted for my pains—not painful though now....

I am learning more and more to be less self-conscious about these things, to feel completely merged in the whole. That is the only thing that enables me—the me that you used to know—to go through some of these things. I have almost no sense of personality at all—it is all group-personality....

Poor Julia has had her wrist in a cast ever since Monday and it is still very painful.

ON THE SAME DAY: Republicans won both houses of Congress, giving them a two-seat majority in the next Senate and a comfortable cushion of fifty votes in the House. On the state suffrage level, Louisiana voted against women's suffrage while Oklahoma voted for it.

On November 7, 1918, a news report from France said the Germans had surrendered. The news was premature, however, and within a few hours had to be corrected. In the meantime, celebrations erupted across the world. People streamed out of offices, factories and homes. According to the *Washington Post*, in the area near Elizabeth, a "Wild Revel...Lasts Till Midnight."

Friday Morning, November 8, 1918

Nothing much to tell, as there have been no activities since Monday except the routine here in the offices and I have been very busy at that. So I will just write a note this morning before going down to breakfast, to keep you from worrying over no word from me.

Washington was truly a wild, wild place yesterday and most of the night, over the rumors of Germany's signing of the Armistice. If anyone wants to believe that the populace as a populace is opposed to peace, let 'em think it—if they can, after a demonstration like yesterday's. But I fear they would be deluding themselves sadly.

It was really marvelous. People seemed beside themselves with joy. When the extra [newspaper special] came out at noon, crowds gathered around the White House and tramped up and down and shouted and waved and hurrahed madly.

Men and women celebrating the end of the war, Washington, D.C. on November 11, 1918. *Library of Congress.*

But the real explosion came in the evening, beginning about seven o'clock and lasting until after midnight. It reminded me of nothing so much as a huge football celebration, a thousand times magnified. Pennsylvania Ave was one great, slow-moving mass, from the Capitol all the way down past the White House to the Army & Navy Building. The crowd all around the Treasury Block was perhaps the densest. And one continual hubbub. Shouts & songs & horns & whistles, until it sounded as though the great human mass with its thousands of waving flags was really Pandemonium broken loose.

Wherever a sufficiently clear space could be found, hundreds of people hung on to each other's coat tails and snake-danced, college fashion, through the streets, chanting as they went. Everything on wheels was out, piled to overflowing, from the smallest cart to the hugest auto-truck, and these went up and down the streets, loaded with soldiers & sailors or government war-workers...

THE REST OF ELIZABETH'S letter is missing.

In Washington, an estimated two hundred thousand people joined in the revelries on the night of November 7—despite official denials of an armistice. No serious injuries were reported in D.C., but in some towns, the combination of crowds, cars and guns proved fatal. And just four days later, on November 11 at eleven o'clock in the morning, peace descended in Europe. The negotiated end to the war was official.

HURRY UP AND WAIT

As NWP suffragist Doris Stevens said of this period:

> *While the United States Senate was standing still under our protest, world events rushed on. German autocracy had collapsed. The Allies had won a military victory. The Kaiser had that very week fled for his life because of the uprising of his people.*
>
> *"We are all free voters of a free republic now," was the message sent by the women of Germany to the women of the United States through Miss Jane Addams. We were at that moment heartily ashamed of our government. German women voting! American women going to jail and spending long hours in the Senate guardhouse without arrests or charges.*[45]

The Senate was out of session and the holidays approaching. NWP work focused on organizing a December member conference, maintaining a stream of communication to supporters and planning provocative new public demonstrations.

Thursday, November 14, 1918

Let's see if I can get busy and answer a few of your letters for the last three or four days before time to dress for the big meeting tonight. I have just come from the office and time is short.

First, you speak of having some misgivings as to the efficacy of our activities here. Don't ever worry on that score. Isn't it all precisely a repetition of what happened last year in the White House picketing—at first good publicity, then none; at first a long period of non-molested action, then the beginning of arrests? And didn't it accomplish its intended result, namely, bringing the President around? We may not be getting any publicity, but don't you worry about the Senate not knowing what we're doing! And it's bound to have its effect, however much they may proclaim to the contrary....

Sunday, November 17, 1918

I was called down earlier than I expected to help get in extra chairs and so this epistle was cut off unduly. Since then I have been spending all my spare time writing campaign letters to help Julia out in her efforts to get picket pledges for next month & several for myself asking for help in raising a small amount of money I pledged. That's my first activity in *that* line!

Last evening I thought *surely* I would get this finished but the addressograph had gone on a rampage & I had a divil [sic] of a time getting it straightened out as I was getting out the last of the *Suffragist* wrappers. And I had been up late so much recently and I was tired, so I tumbled into bed at 9:30 instead.

This morning I was terribly industrious: washed my tan checked dress (and will have it pressed—cleaning would have broke me flat) and some underthings, mended two pairs of stockings, and wrote

Edith Ainge, the "Angel" of NWP headquarters. From the "Prison Tour" of formerly jailed suffragists. 1919. *Library of Congress.*

two more letters. I felt almost insufferably virtuous. Everyone on the floor came in to view my good works.

Our household Guardian Angel [Edith Ainge] is going away tonight, to New York to take care of her sick brother, and we'll miss her like the mischief. She always binds up the hurted ones & tucks in the homesick ones at night & kisses us good morning and goes places with us. But she'll be back.

A bunch of us had lunch with her this noon, I've just come from it. Yum, it was a good lunch! But I'm lucky to be getting meals at $10 a week in this town. I just figured up my today's lunch from the prices on the menu, that the poor public pays, and it came to 90 cents: fruit salad (a delicious big one, though), 50¢; glass of milk, 10¢; homemade gingerbread, 15¢; and baked apple, 15¢....

We've been having the windows wide open all day today (what beautiful repetition!) and there's been a gentle, warm little rain, almost like Spring. Wish somebody felt like going out for a tramp in the rain with me, but nobody does.

Oh dear! Aingy's going to be away for Thanksgiving, and Berthe Arnold, and Jamie's going home, and Julia is and doesn't want to, and I want to and can't! Poor Julia's trips home are anything but pleasant....[46]

What would you say if I cut off my hair? When I see how free and comfortable Jamie is and so many others, I almost want to. If I didn't remember the bushy fright of younger bobbed hair design days I almost might! I just wondered what you would do to me....

I'd be glad to have you send copies of those "compilations" [extracts of Elizabeth's letters] you had made, as *coming from you not me*, to the following [six people]...

Just say that they might be interested in some parts of my letters to you, as showing what I am doing. I want to attack them myself later from a different angle. But it will be well for them to have this background....

Goodnight, my dear, for this time. Will all the love in the world, Elizabeth

Tuesday, November 19, 1918

Dear Folks:

Today I paid my first month's bills of fifty-five dollars, board and rent. Last year [in Chicago] I was only paying thirty-two a month, $12 for room and $5 a week for board. Rather a jump, isn't it? But even so, I pay less than half the average room rent, and about a third less for my meals, by the rate of $10 a week.

Gee! This has seemed like a lone five days since hearing from anyone! I know I haven't any right to kick, for my letters have had to be few and far between lately. While my days were mostly filled with activities it was a rest & relief and a necessary safety valve to write, as well as a pleasure. But now I find that it has been put in the luxury class, for it seems to me that I do nothing *but* write. So far as the mechanical operation is concerned, and when any hours off arrive, I either just *must* do something else or else tumble into bed.

What do you think I did this evening for recreation? Went to a class in Criminal Law at Jamie's Law School, the National University![47] She has evening classes, several nights a week. This is the first year the National has admitted women....[48]

Would you send me...maybe one or two of my pennants for my room, Texas? Rice?...

Vivian Pierce. Date unknown. *Library of Congress.*

There are to be regular Thursday night meetings here from now on. Miss Younger is to speak at the next one. I wish the *Suffragist* this week had carried *all* of Miss Paul's speech just as she said it....

Vivian Pierce is back. The ones [*Suffragists*] while she was in New Jersey were rather poor. She goes away again tomorrow though, to campaign in Louisiana.

You ought to know Vivian. She's the most unusual person I've ever met. Wonderfully keen and witty and funny, but awfully biting and cynical when she wants to be. She's unusual-looking, too. She's part East-Indian; her mother was a Parsee. (Which always reminds me of the old Parsee who baked cakes on the shore of the sea in which the rhinoceros bathed, first taking off his skin which buttoned neatly up the back, while the sun shone with more-than-Oriental splendor.)[49]

With which I shall retire. Elizabeth

Sunday, November 24, 1918

Dear Mother:

[After discussing acquaintances who might be asked for donations:] Other names you mention I have on my *Suffragist* list and do not want to ask more than the subscription. Of the two, the subscription is really the more valuable because it widens our news circle. Each one of us here at Headquarters was asked to pledge only a small amount, as we have our regular work here and there are others who are devoting their time to that among the branch organizations.

I wrote twelve letters, though, some of them necessarily rather long, which is all I have been able to do....Am trying to make slow headway with my subscription letters, but so far have not sent off more than a half dozen or so, as there has been almost no time off from routine work and that is of such a detailed nature that I *daren't* get behind without danger of becoming hopelessly muddled....

Lorna [a friend from Texas] would be a good one for the demonstration if not for her *Ideas*. She's really terribly conservative at heart, in spite of her progressiveness in many things, you know. Of course it's her father's influence, mainly, but that's inbred.

Hope the letters from you may possibly have some effect. I was really quite a little hurt at a letter from her (tho' I realize that it's only her lack of knowledge of the first thing about the matter which is responsible) in which she said, "What were the women arrested for? If it was for picketing the White House they got just what they deserved."

Coming home from a rather bad experience at the Capitol to a letter like that from a friend, I was just a little bit too angry to attempt writing an answer or offering a vindication. I don't like this business of offering a vindication for *any action of ours* that called forth the sort of beastly but *unquestioned actions* of the police. I don't particularly care about apologizing to people for fighting their fight for them. Of course I know she doesn't understand and it's up to me to *make* her—but why *shouldn't a woman of her intelligence understand without being shown?*

Of course many intelligent women may question the *efficiency* of the methods until they had been made to see the reason underlying Alice Paul's unusually sane tactics. But to question the *principle*, the *right*—! Or to feel anything but indignation over the treatment that has been accorded us—not as *us* but as American *citizens*—!

Heaven knows we are not asking special privilege as women, but the same right to petition as men have and the very same treatment that would be given men in our position. They make loud threats about what they would do to us if we were men, but they know they lie. They would not and never did *dare* treat men citizens as we have been treated.[50]

Very, very early in the present campaign, when the rough stuff was still quite mild, one infuriated officer made to Mrs. Moller the time-honored remark, between his teeth, "I wish you were a *man!*" To which Mrs. Moller replied instantly, "I wish *you* were!"

But I have gotten way, way off the subject.

Someday when I'm feeling just primed, I'll write to Miss Lorna. If I didn't love her and know she really cared for me I would not be hurt, for heavens knows that I am aware of the many, many people in this world who do not think as I do and who are at perfect liberty to disagree—until we've had time to convert 'em!

If only women would stop thinking of the vote as merely a *right*, an end only—a duty which they themselves did not particularly

Bertha Moller, circa 1919.
Library of Congress.

care to bother with—and look upon Equal Suffrage as a *principle*, something without which as a foundation none of the other great reforms of a forward-thinking democratic people can come about! It's not an end! It's a means to an end.

And by that I do not mean that with women voting all the other reforms will immediately spring into being. Of course not. I mean simply that there are a great many reforms which must be worked for—reforms of labor, reforms of politics, reforms of education, reforms of government itself—and all these looking to a higher democracy. And that the first of these, the essential, the only thing which in itself will give a democratic foundation that is *not* spurious, on which to build, is the working principle of *universal equal* suffrage, unabridged and unrestricted. When we have got that, then we can begin and work for something else.

Probably you are saying, "Why don't you go ahead and write all this first hand as one of your 'convert' letters, instead of to me first, when I believe it all already?"

Well, you see, I have to. It's all inside me and, as an unformulated mass, I know it. But before I can write it I have to really think it out for myself just whenever I feel like boiling over or bursting. I have to formulate it before I can see it and I can't think it out to anyone but you.

No, of course I didn't mean I am "broke." I simply meant that they charge such outrageous prices for cleaning that once or twice would buy a new dress and I couldn't afford it. I have all my months bills paid and $40 in the bank....

There's never any danger of running out of funds. And if I did for any urgent reason, the Treasurer would tide me over. No one is wealthy around here or ashamed of scraping pennies, for all extra money goes to the cause.

Was not hurt in last raid. Mrs. Kelly had only been in one other picket and knew nothing about it when she said it was the roughest arrest ever. Dear me, those *rude* policemen!

This "note" is like Woody's, it has no end. Now, in haste, to get to the point I really meant to write of. Your introduction to the compilation for the President's consumption is simply *splendid*, I think, quiet and dignified and reserved and yet sufficiently protestant. I wish we could have some way of knowing how it actually does fare.

And now I have an idea. I am returning the copy you sent me and I want you to mail it direct to Alice Paul as letting her know what you've done, and as though you had not consulted me. I know she will be pleased because she has been wanting people to protest to Wilson. But it will make a better impression if she thinks I had nothing to do with it and if she thereby knows that my letters were not written for the purpose. I have a reason, and believe me, I know little A.P. well enough to know that it will work out! Just send directly back to her as it is....

Heaps of love, Elizabeth

Increasing the Pressure

On December 2, 1918, Wilson included a call to pass the suffrage amendment in his annual address to Congress. Despite this, the NWP continued targeting him as head of the party in power.

Bits of Elizabeth's letters focus on Christmas shopping for friends and family. One addressed her mother's concern that she was calling a friend

Berthe Arnold checking a watchfire in front of NWP headquarters. 1919. *Library of Congress.*

from college by his first name. Elizabeth first stated she thought it all "prudery and nonsense" not to use first names with friends. But, she added, she would never want to hurt him. She appreciated her mother's comment that perhaps her manner was becoming too familiar.

From December 12 to 16, the NWP held a conference in Washington. In a postcard from December 10, Elizabeth mentioned, "I have gotten quite all right again, but head over heels in work. Office and conference work too, for the end of this week. That's what kept me from writing."

The conference included finalizing plans for a watchfire campaign at the White House to start January 1. And the women held a massive demonstration on December 16, the day that Wilson arrived in France for the Paris Peace Conference.

According to the NWP press release, "Miss Mary Ingham, Pa. state chairman, pointed out that Wilson's words would not only be burned up, but their inconsistency would be burned into the minds of the American public."

Doris Stevens reported:[51]

> Less than fifty legislative days remained to us. Something had to be done quickly, something bold and offensive enough to threaten the prestige of the President, as he was riding in sublimity to unknown heights as a champion of world liberty.…It was unanimously decided to light a fire in an urn, and, on the day that the President was officially received by France, to burn with fitting public ceremonies all the President's past and present speeches or books concerning "liberty," "freedom" and "democracy."
>
> It was late afternoon when the four hundred women proceeded solemnly in single file from headquarters, past the White House, along the edge of the quiet and beautiful Lafayette Park, to the foot of Lafayette's statue. A slight mist added beauty to the pageant. The purple, white and gold banners, so brilliant in the sunshine, became soft pastel sails. Half the procession carried lighted torches; the other half banners.…
>
> The torch was applied to the pine-wood logs in the Grecian Urn at the edge of the broad base of the statue. As the flames began to mount, Vida Milholland stepped forward and without accompaniment sang again from that spot of beauty, in her own challenging way, the Woman's Marseillaise. Even the small boys in the crowd, always the most difficult to please, cheered and clapped and cried for more.
>
> Mrs. John Rogers, Jr., chairman of the National Advisory Council, said, as president of the ceremony: "We hold this meeting to protest against the denial of liberty to American women. All over the world to-day we

see surging and sweeping irresistibly on, the great tide of democracy, and women would be derelict in their duty if they did not see to it that it brings freedom to the women of this land...."

The casual observer said, "They must be crazy. Don't they know the President isn't at home? Why are they appealing to him in the park opposite the White House when he is in France?" The long line of bright torches shone menacingly as the women marched slowly back to headquarters, and the crowd dispersed in silence. The White House was empty. But we knew our message would be heard in France.

New Year, More Jail

The watchfires began in earnest on January 1, 1919, in front of the White House. The NWP wanted to embarrass the president, still in France, into pushing his party to pass suffrage. Edith Ainge lit the urn while Mary Dubrow and Annie Arniel unfurled a banner: "President Wilson is deceiving the world when he appears as the prophet of democracy."

Almost immediately, furious onlookers overturned the fire. The suffragists started another fire in Lafayette Square, and those suffragists were briefly arrested. Meanwhile, the White House fire urn was relit. And they kept relighting it.

Multiple fire locations were eventually used by the NWP: an urn in front of headquarters, then sites in front of the White House and in Lafayette Square. Even rain did not deter the demonstrations and the fires.

Kerosene was the secret to long-lasting fires. A good soaking ensured wood kept burning despite bad weather or crowd attacks. According to Inez Irwin:

Everything and everybody smelled of kerosene. All the time, there was one room in which logs were kept soaking in this pervasive fluid. When they first started the Watchfires they carried the urn and the oil-soaked logs openly, to the appointed spot on the pavement in front of the White House. Later, when the arrests began and the fires had to be built so swiftly that they had to abandon the urn, they carried these logs under coats or capes.[52]

The January audiences, despite the cold, were probably larger than normal. The White House, while the president was away, reopened the lower level to the public. This was a return to the prewar openness fondly remembered by

Despite the weather, picketers carried on with watchfire demonstration in front of the White House. January 2, 1919. *Library of Congress.*

NWP's bell at headquarters, hung in 1919 to ring out whenever Wilson's words were burned—until an angry crowd tore it down. 1919. *Library of Congress.*

At a January watchfire demonstration, two suffragists hold a banner blaming President Wilson for women's lack of suffrage. 1919. *Library of Congress.*

many local residents. With war workers and soldiers winding down work and returning home, access to the White House was a special treat.

For even more suffrage attention, the NWP rigged up a bell on the balcony outside the headquarters. When a new Wilson speech was transmitted from Paris, the bell would ring out. Then women would gather and march over to the urn. With great fanfare, they would throw Wilson's speech into the fire.

Elizabeth went for a break after the December conference. But she was back by January. On the sixth, she was in a District courtroom to support NWP members who had been arrested at a watchfire, including Alice Paul, Julia Emory, Mary Dubrow, Annie Arniel and two others. They refused to listen to the judge or to defend themselves, were fined and refused to pay and received five- to ten-day jail sentences.[53]

January 6, 1919

Dear Mother...

You ought to see how rosy this cold weather is making my cheeks now that I am in such good condition....Zero, snow & sleighs! Brr-r-r!! It's really been quite cold enough here this past week, biting cold. The snow only lasted a few hours though....

The crowd quickly starts to gather around the suffragists standing against the fence. Watchfire demonstration, 1919. *Library of Congress.*

The trapped feeling of picketing: an unnamed suffragist surrounded by a crowd, her back against the White House fence. Dated 1917. *Library of Congress.*

The watchfire was kicked apart by the crowd or police. 1919. *Library of Congress.*

Police swept the scattered logs into the gutter. 1919. *Library of Congress.*

A suffragist plucked out a burning log to start again. The NWP soaked the wood in kerosene to ensure it kept burning. 1919. *Library of Congress.*

Police start taking suffragists to the police van, through a dense but not unfriendly crowd. Only the suffrage banners are visible. 1919. *Library of Congress.*

Suffragist being marched to the paddy wagon. 1919. *Library of Congress.*

I'm pretty tired tonight, after a full day in Courtroom and office, so as I've said about all there is to be said, I'll have my bath and go to bed...Goodnight, Elizabeth

Think how narrowly you have just escaped the disgrace of having a jail-bird daughter!

BUT ELIZABETH DIDN'T ESCAPE for long. On January 13, she and twenty-one others were arrested at the watchfire. Refusing bail, they were sentenced to five days in the D.C. Jail. The following letter was written after she got out, having been taken back to NWP headquarters in an ambulance.

January 18, 1919

Home again.

My dear Folks: I didn't write on Friday because I had no way of getting letter out [from jail], and I had about lost all interest in the world anyhow. Yesterday I couldn't—as I will explain later. But by this afternoon I can sit up about five minutes at a time, so I think I can a letter write, though it's apt to be disconnected.

Monday, January 19, 1919

Well, I seem to have made a mistake yesterday about how long I could sit up. Someone sent a wire for me the first thing this morning when I woke up, though, so you wouldn't worry until you got this letter. I guess someone asked me last evening if I wanted to send any, but I must not have answered.

Well, now, I will try and tell you the whole story, as well as I remember it. I am not trying to sit up, I have my paper propped up in front of me, so unless I get too tired I can go straight ahead and tell it all.

I stayed in bed all day Friday [in jail], partly to keep away from the rabble downstairs. (I can't let myself think of all that even yet without sort of losing my balance.)

In the evening when I got down from my upper bunk for a minute I got dizzy and faint and had to rest a bit on Jamie's bed before I was able to climb up into mine. Jamie got scared and went to Miss Chevier for her smelling salts. Miss C. came back and said she knew if I'd let her give me a bath I'd feel refreshed. So she took me down stairs to the bath room (I had gone down once the day before and fallen out backward by sheer force of repulsion at the awful conditions) but she had found one corner which was cleaned out a little and had an overhead shower. So she undressed me and stood me on newspapers and gave me a quick going over and a rub down, which did feel good.

Then I remember coming up stairs with my arms around her neck and wondering half way up if I could ever get up the last few. That's all I do remember except everything getting black and that I slumped down very heavily on her shoulder. She said she called some women downstairs and they carried me into our cell and put me on Jamie's bed, and when I came to, Miss Ainge was there by me rubbing my chest and forehead and hands.

⁓

Well, a good deal of time has gone since I wrote the above. I seem to be refreshed and strengthened, and then to have periods of depression when I can do nothing but lie perfectly inert and it's all I can do to breathe and notice people. The weakness seemed to have been too much for my heart at the last, and it having all it could do to keep pumping at all was overtaxed by that trip upstairs, and the fainting came to relieve it. I think it was all due more to lack of air than anything else.

I have felt just as I imagined one would from what they call "oxygen starvation." I have had to breathe by deep gulps ever since I came out. That I know, rather than lack of food, is what starved the heart of fuel. You know I have often fasted for several days when not feeling well (but with plenty of outdoor air and exercise), and had no such trouble, nor even lost strength. But conditions there—you can't *believe*—but no more of jail now—

Saturday, when I came out, my heart pounded so slowly and hard that it shook my whole body. I could touch my finger lightly on any spot on my body and feel the pulse thump-thump. Especially in my throat, where it tightened and constricted my breathing. But now that has stopped and as long as I am perfectly still in bed the heavy pounding is not so agonizing.

I was brought home in an ambulance. They tell me they had to fight for an hour and a half after release time with [superintendent of D.C. jails] Zinkhan[54] to get it. I had slept practically none that night and had collapsed again partially during that time. They had left our cell and Miss Chevier's unlocked so she could look after me and she was with me often. I couldn't even be lifted up to a sitting posture without something inside of me cutting off my breath at once.

In that interminable grey morning I have hazy recollections of Aingy sitting beside me in the cell and holding my hand after the rest had gone down to the door. And of hearing someone say that Miss (Lucy) Burns [NWP leader] refused to let anyone leave until Zinkhan brought an ambulance for me. And then the last thing that I remember at all was Miss Burn's voice saying at last, "Here they are," of being lifted out of bed onto what was evidently a stretcher by two tobacco-y guards and a very onion-y one—of a rather precarious floating sense for a long while, then a rush of air into my lungs, then nothing except an occasional rumble.[55]

Then sometime or other I opened my eyes to my own little room, with someone feeding me spoonsful of orange juice. Oh, the heavenly softness of my little cot!! The inexpressible delight of fresh breezes streaming in thru open windows! And the *quiet!*

But you want to know about my condition. It seems to me I'm apt to get rather mixed up. It seems they brought a doctor in right away and that everybody was terrible frightened. I don't remember much about the Doctor's visit, but part I heard them repeat to Mrs. Branham[56] later, and part Matilda told me. (Matilda made herself my nurse that day.) He was a young Doctor and asked all about my condition, and took my pulse, and used a stethoscope—isn't?—on my chest. He told them that the things liable to happen to me were acute gastritis or a slight dilation, from forced or too much feeding.

That sounded promising, *but* he went on to say that I should have thick beef broth every two hours, then two doses of oat meal gruel; then on Sunday chicken broth every three hours, and by night a soft poached egg and a piece of toast; by Monday I might have what I liked. No orange juice or grapefruit for three days—acids very dangerous to the stomach in such a condition. (We know what such feeding would have done to me.)

When I collapsed on Mrs. Branham's hands yesterday after I started this letter, and they all got frightened about me because I lay without rousing for a long while getting over the effects of the disturbance, someone, Mrs. Weed I think, got panicky and called in another doctor. And this one said—"Orange juice—fine. Give her all she wants of it."

Speaking of doctors, the one that came in to me at the jail Friday night after I had collapsed, said I would *have* to have stimulant or my heart would not last until morning—and then was so terribly interested that he forgot to bring it back! Of course, knowing the danger of it, I would not have taken it if he had—but it just goes to show.

But to get back to the first doctor. After he had gone and she heard about it, Miss Younger rushed to my rescue and said it was all nonsense—that she had no faith in that young thing, that she has gotten over the flu on orange juice—that I craved it and therefore I should have it. Matilda said she thought so too, and between them they agreed to stand by me and keep others from trying to make me eat the stuff. I was much too weak to have made much resistance, I know.

So I was left to my orange juice, and later a half grapefruit. By night my slight fever was gone (I had a pack for it one night in jail)—and by next morning I was able to feed myself and to know all that was going on around me. I rested quietly all morning, only raising my head occasionally in an experimental fashion. As I say, the heart thumping had very much moderated.

I think I have now reached the point at which this letter was started, Sunday. I tried to sit propped up just a very few moments— and suddenly something stopped inside, and over I went. Mrs. Branham must have found me almost immediately from what I can gather and laid me down flat again. I don't think I entirely lost consciousness, but I have the very haziest idea of the rest of the afternoon. They say they kept someone with me sitting near all the time.

I remember people moving about sometimes, and bending over me, and once someone (it turned out to be Miss Younger) rubbed my back and kneaded it, which felt awfully good. Then it seems that Mrs. Moller (she had ridden home with me in the ambulance and was worried anyway) came in to speak to me and I was so inert, and looked at her without seeing her, and she said, "My child, don't you know me?" and began to weep and hurried out. And Mrs. Weed had called to me from the door with the same result and they both rushed to Miss Paul and told her I was dying, and Mrs. Wood sent for the second doctor.

I don't remember any of this, but this is what they told me. I just know that I was struggling all the while for big, deep breaths and that my body felt like a big hollow drum with my heart beating heavily against it. Of course it was just a semi-faint condition which came as a relief to the over-worked state of affairs when my heart was having to pump uphill.

Well, I was aroused by the Angel's (Miss Ainge) voice. She got up here before even Mrs. Moller could get back; and had everyone quieted, sat down by my bed, and I looked up and saw her at once. She smiled at me and I remembered everything from then on, though I was still too weak to say anything. And you ought to hear her talk once and see her smile. You have to smile right back, even if you are dead.

Tuesday Morning

This letter has been a long slow process, hasn't it? It had to be written in little bits. I didn't want to send it half finished for fear you'd be frightened, and I just couldn't get it done. I felt much stronger and more alive last night, though, and still better this morning—oh so much. Now I will try to finish this up, even if sketchily, and get it mailed.

The new doctor appeared (though Aingy stoutly maintained that we didn't want one) just after I had finished a supper of spinach and lettuce and he said they were the finest things in the world for me—also the orange juice; and next day to alternate every hour (one) the juice of two oranges and (two) milk, with later a little bit of raw egg. This sounded very sensible, and I thought I probably needed it, so yesterday I followed that with the addition of a little fresh lettuce and cooked spinach at night. I didn't really have that much food, either, because I have only been able to take a very little at a time and I wasn't hungry that often. I don't think I had more than two glasses of milk all day.

That night Aingy gave me a sponge bath in bed and a gentle rubbing all over and put me into clean clothes. I had not been able to have my horribly smelly jail ones off yet. She had been in bed all day herself. She has bathed me and rubbed me and combed my hair and fed regularly ever since. I can eat by myself again today though, and this morning I sat up in an easy chair while they made my bed up fresh.

If you only know how wonderful everybody in the place has been to me! I simply cannot begin to express it to you now, but someday I will tell you. Miss Ainge and Miss Burns are to go out on the Prison special soon, and if it comes to Chicago or Columbus you must see them somehow.

There are so many things I have inside my head that I can't get out onto paper yet, so I'm only making this a letter to reassure you about me. I am truly going to take the best of care of myself and go at things very easily.

Sunday when I first started my letter I meant to tell you that I had a bowl of the sweetest, loveliest big pansies by my bedside, that Miss Wood had brought me. We have had three days of glorious warm, breezy sunny weather streaming in my two windows since I came back.

I will not write more now. In a day or two I will write a letter that will have more of interest to people outside the family, about jail and all the other current activities.

Chapter 3

WATCHFIRES AND VICTORY

A round this time, Elizabeth's mother moved to Washington, D.C., and no more letters were saved. From other sources, we know Elizabeth stayed on at NWP. Her work remained a combination of picketing, publishing and other assignments.

The watchfires continued to burn, and suffragists continued to be arrested and jailed. One news report said that Clara Wold and Mildred Morris had planned to go to Paris and hold watchfires at the Paris Peace Conference. According to the report, their passports were "withdrawn" by the State Department. This story may have been part of the NWP strategy to keep pressure on the president, threatening to follow Wilson wherever he might go.[57]

One of the most dramatic NWP demonstrations took place just a few weeks after Elizabeth's last letter to her mother. In its final session, on February 10, the Democrat-controlled Senate was to vote again on the suffrage bill. The newly-elected, Republican-controlled Senate would start in May.

Paul pushed the outgoing Democrats to claim a suffrage victory before the Republicans could do so. Most importantly, she wanted Wilson to press them also. He was still in France but in regular contact via telegram, cable and the media.

On February 9, the night before the vote, women streamed out of NWP headquarters and up to the White House. Over the watchfire, they burned a straw-stuffed paper effigy of the president, in front of an aghast crowd. While the war was over, the shock value of this effort was substantial.

Another day, another protest. Mary Dubrow is speaking, and Elizabeth stands on the far right. Circa 1919. *Library of Congress.*

The picketers were arrested and jailed. The women refused to eat and started a hunger strike. As in other arrests, they claimed "political prisoner" status. After four days, the women were released. The vote in the Senate had failed again, and Wilson remained an NWP target.

In late February, the president arrived home via Boston for a brief visit. He was reporting to Congress and then returning via New York to Paris. In Boston, before Wilson even had a chance to see them, picketing NWP women were arrested. When they refused to pay fines for an "illegal gathering," they were sentenced to eight days in jail.

On March 4, as Wilson headed back to the peace talks, six NWP women were detained in New York City. At the time, they were assembling in front of the Metropolitan Opera House where Wilson was to speak later. When the women were released without charges, a mob of onlookers—soldiers and civilians—attacked them. Police eventually broke up the disturbance.

Back in Washington, the new Congress began its first session in May 1919. The House again passed the suffrage bill, and attention quickly turned to the Senate. Finally, on June 4, 1919, the Senate passed the Susan B. Anthony

Julia Emory and Bertha Graf carrying bundles of banners, preparing for another trip to support ratification. July 20, 1920. National Photo Company. *Library of Congress.*

Amendment. Celebrations! Tears! Across the city and the country, for all the suffragists in all the organizations!

Yet Senate approval was not the final goal, and immediately, the suffragists were deep in work again. Before women's suffrage became law, at least thirty-six of forty-eight states must ratify the amendment. Many more political battles ensued, but at statehouses rather than in Washington.

Time was of the essence if women were to vote in the November 1920 presidential election. Not all states had legislative sessions upcoming, so they had to agree to call special sessions. The Eighteenth Amendment, the Prohibition Act, took just over one year to ratify. Could the more controversial Nineteenth Amendment match that?

Some states were a given, ready to vote as soon as the Senate acted. In the first week, Michigan and Wisconsin ratified the amendment. Texas, the first southern state to ratify, passed the bill a few weeks later.

Elizabeth and her mother, Benigna, had the honor of delivering the ratification papers to the U.S. secretary of state in Washington.[58] And Elizabeth finally cut her hair. The NWP press release showed her in a short bob and provided this quote:

> *The day of the short-haired woman will soon be here in reality....I cut mine for convenience sake and under no circumstances would I let it grow long again. My head feels better, I am rid of hair pins, I don't have to hang my head out the window over the fire escape for hours to dry my hair when I wash it. Men got onto this centuries ago, but women are adopting it with their new freedom.*[59]

Left: Elizabeth Kalb, circa 1920. She enjoyed the fashionable "cropped hair" sported by other suffragists she met. *Library of Congress.*

Opposite, top: NWP members hold a protest banner at the GOP Convention. June 1920. *Library of Congress.*

Opposite, bottom: The NWP snuck a banner into the 1920 GOP Convention in Chicago. "We don't want planks. We demand the 36th State [Ratification]." *Library of Congress.*

By summer 1920, thirty-five states had ratified and eight rejected the amendment. Only five states remained to vote, and one more yes was desperately needed. Women had little time to get registered if suffrage did not pass soon.

While activity was concentrated in the states, Elizabeth's job was largely in Washington. Publications and correspondence had to be prepared, produced and distributed. A fire at headquarters on January 7, 1920, did not help. First the boiler and then a stack of coal caught fire. No one was hurt, but the smoke and hose water must have made sleeping and working difficult.

Elizabeth did leave town for at least one event: the June 1920 Republican convention in Chicago. The NWP lobbied politicians from states that had not yet ratified, while also demanding that suffrage be part of the Republican platform. And well-prepared NWP members brought banners with them. They picketed the convention and hung a large banner demanding suffrage over the heads of the delegates.

Despite these efforts, the GOP did not add suffrage to its platform. Less than three weeks later, the Democratic National Convention opened in San Francisco. The Democratic Party expressed support for ratification and included a suffrage plank in its platform. After the conventions ended, NWP members met with presidential nominees and continued targeting states for ratification.

So for just over a year, until August 18, 1920, volunteers and staff of NWP, NAWSA and other organizations petitioned, cajoled and pressured state politicians. Finally, on a hot summer day in Tennessee, a "certain no"

NWP celebrating at headquarters. Alice Paul is above with the "Ratification" flag: a star for each state that voted yes. August 1920. *Library of Congress.*

senator voted yes, and the amendment was ratified by a thirty-sixth state. The fight for federal legal protection of women's suffrage was over.

More formally, the amendment was approved by the state legislature on August 18, certified by the governor on the twenty-fourth and finally certified by U.S. Secretary of State Bainbridge Colby on August 25. Colby received the amendment at night and chose to sign it the next morning. No suffragists or special guests were present. Alice Paul requested that the event be re-created and filmed, but this was rejected.

Chapter 4

WHAT NEXT?

An ending and a beginning in one, the Nineteenth Amendment was now official. NWP's laser-focused staff and volunteers had to grapple with their new future. Their sole objective had been this constitutional amendment, to guarantee women's right to vote and thus fully participate in the operation of local, state and federal governments.

NAWSA resolved this question of "What next?" by establishing the League of Women Voters. The league's goal was education, encouraging participation and ensuring that women received nonpartisan information on their choices. Unlike the centralized power structure used in the last years of the NAWSA campaign, local league chapters controlled decision-making and membership.

NWP faced both practical and philosophical decisions. First, the practical: how to celebrate their success and when to close the Jackson Place headquarters. The landlord had been trying for months to have them removed from the premises for overstaying the lease—so leaving was essential! And philosophically: whether to end the National Woman's Party or keep the organization but with a new goal.

To address the practical, the NWP planned a February 1921 members' conference, the sale of furnishings and equipment immediately after this event and a move with smaller staff to new quarters on Capitol Hill. The NWP's major funder, Alva Belmont, made this move possible.

Elizabeth stayed with the NWP through the conference. Her work included helping organize the conference and creating educational pieces for new

Three Generations Of Suffragists

From left to right are Mrs. Elizabeth Park Green, 78 years old; Mrs. Benigan Kalb, 48, and Miss Elizabeth Green Kalb, 23, grandmother, mother and daughter, all of whom are delegates to the convention of the National Woman's Party now being held in Washington. Mrs. Green, of Columbus, Ohio, mother of seven children, was a war worker during the Civil and World Wars and has been a suffragist for many years. She led the suffrage delegation to see President-elect Harding at Marion, Ohio, last summer. Mrs. Kalb, of Texas, has been vice-chairman of the Texas branch of the Woman's Party since its organization. Miss Kalb has been active in demonstrations of the Woman's Party.

Elizabeth with her mother and grandmother, both suffragists. All three attended the 1921 NWP conference. *The* Baltimore Sun, *February 16, 1921.*

voters. Without picketing, Elizabeth had time for another passion: music. She joined the newly formed Washington Community Opera Company.[60]

A celebration of victory, the conference was also Alice Paul's opportunity to set a new course for the organization. For her, the philosophical question was already answered. She wanted the NWP to focus on equal rights.

NWP staff and members fell into three general camps: those who wanted to relax or live a "normal" life after years of hard-fought campaigning, those with one or more other issues to pursue (international disarmament, child welfare, racial equality, etc.) and those who believed suffrage was not yet won if women were unable to vote due to ignorance or restrictions. These different views were reflected in the conference, along with the desire to celebrate their suffrage success.

Some people expected a broad discussion at the conference on what to do next. After all, an NWP mailing had specifically asked: "If a new program is undertaken, what shall it be? We ask each member of the Woman's Party to come to the convention to advise as to the next step, or to send her views through a delegate."[61] And even before the conference started, diverse people and groups appealed to Alice Paul for attention to their issues.

But a strong leader has this advantage: no need to listen to everyone, just to ensure that enough people are willing to go along with the plan. Alice Paul and the executive committee met in the months before the conference to draft a "next step" proposal. Women must be completely equal under the law, Alice Paul counseled, already planning her next fight. Full equality must be guaranteed in all aspects of life: marriage, education, employment, etc.

At the conference, discussion gave way to pushing through the committee's proposal. While the majority present voted for the new focus—equal rights—a significant number of women felt shunted aside and unheard. This included some supporters of the committee's minority report, proposing the NWP work for immediate world disarmament.[62]

Yet the structure and the culture of the organization had always centered on single-issue advocacy and Alice Paul's vision. That she chose another fundamental right as the NWP's goal was not surprising. Paul wanted an association dedicated to gaining women's rights—not to world peace or good government or even enforcement of newly created rights.

After the conference, the NWP focused on passing the Equal Rights Amendment and on supporting women's rights internationally. And Elizabeth? She showed no interest in staying on at the NWP. As she described it, looking back several years later:

[O]n the Eastern coast, Mother had joined me from her own professional life in the middle West, at about the time I was released from those last hectic years of suffrage struggle in the revered Capital of our Nation. There, looking toward the future, we pooled our reactions, our ideas, and our little dreams—and we voted unanimously for PEACE. Peace at any price!

Then we pooled our capital—if what I had to pool could be so dignified. And we fared forth across the world—it almost seemed like that—from Atlantic to Pacific, in search of—cessation. Cessation of everything active and formidable and commanding. And for this haven whither we were bent I had numerous qualificational demands, but the chief one was that there should be no telephone extension at my bedside.

(I did not, as might have been expected, make any qualification concerning alarm-clocks—because for years clocks had meant nothing in my life! The night was as day and the day night; "Suffragist" copy and printing press forms, political exigencies, bannered demonstrations and prison cells—all these have a peculiar, spurning disregard of clocks, with their petty, ordered minutes and hours.)

Elizabeth and her mother took the train west, to join her father in California. Before leaving Washington, however, Elizabeth joined the Women's Committee for Disarmament. International relations became a major focus of her work life. She also believed in the Equal Rights Amendment, according to an article she wrote in 1931.[63]

Elizabeth never regretted her time in Washington. As she noted later, suffrage taught her:

So long as people said "Please" too long and too meekly they never got anything, but when they grew earnest enough and well-informed enough and said "We Demand..."—they usually got what they demanded—after, of course, careful organization, detailed and widespread propaganda, far-visioned planning, refusal to be discouraged, etc., etc.

The Final Irony

Could Elizabeth vote in 1920? Not if her residence was Washington, D.C., where she had lived for over two years. Despite passage of the Nineteenth Amendment, residents of the District of Columbia still had no political voice. Even the city council was appointed, not elected.

All is forgiven? Alice Paul shakes hands with Assistant Superintendent Daniel Sullivan of the Metropolitan Police Department, circa 1920. *Library of Congress.*

The *Washington Times*, on November 2, 1920, claimed that an estimated two hundred thousand women in D.C. were unable to vote. But the NWP had already highlighted these difficulties in August, immediately after ratification. First, they wanted the expense of train tickets reduced for women traveling to their residence to vote. They claimed that was a custom previously and should continue—but reported that rail officials "just laughed."[64]

Second, the NWP described the difficulty many D.C. women faced based on their legal residence. Some were war workers who had listed the District as their residence when taking the civil service exam—and now were stuck with no suffrage.

But married women were the most constrained. Their residence was that of their husband. If he had a home only in Washington, his wife was also a resident of the city and had no vote. One solution for single women who could afford it: buy property in Maryland or Virginia as soon as possible to establish a nearby residence. But for married women at NWP headquarters:

> *With the single exception of Mrs. Bengina [sic] Green Kalb, who is also secretary of the National Farm Women's Congress, not one of them, despite their long fight for the ballot, will be able to vote, and all on account of their husbands. "Our husbands are disenfranchised because they have no other place of residence than Washington and so we must lose our vote too," said Mrs. Elinor Marsh, assistant editor of the Suffragist. "It is unjust. Married women should be permitted to establish legal residence."*[65]

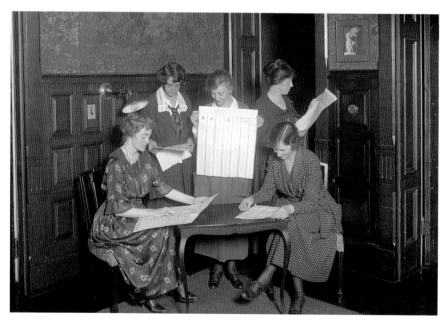

At NWP headquarters, women look over 1920 election ballots. Elizabeth is standing second from left. *Library of Congress.*

Although residing in the District, Elizabeth may have voted in Texas or Ohio. If her parents still owned property in Texas, she might have used that state for residency, or she might have used her father's address in Ohio. Elizabeth's mother continued to claim that she was "of Houston," although she had not lived there since 1916. Benigna was qualified to vote anywhere her husband was living in a state outside D.C.

Alice Paul apparently voted, although she had lived in D.C. since 1914. On September 6, a newspaper report stated that "Miss Paul is voteless" due to her seven-year residence in Washington.[66] Then, late in October, newspapers reported that Paul had filed to vote in New Jersey, her prior home. Ironically, she had help from President Wilson. He commissioned NWP activist Katherine Finnagan (per the newspaper report, but most likely this was NWP activist Catherine Flanagan, visiting D.C. at the time) as a notary to certify her papers.[67]

And over one hundred years later? D.C. residents still have only limited suffrage. In 1961, District residents won the right to vote in presidential elections. They have a nonvoting congressional representative and no Senate representation. A request for help in obtaining D.C. voting rights was rejected at the 1921 NWP conference.[68]

Historic change rarely comes with a bright-line ending and a single image. There is much more to the suffrage story.

Chapter 5

WHO'S MISSING

Suffrage, like other American social movements, was deeply affected by race and class. Some people were not allowed to participate, some are not remembered as having participated and some were excluded from benefits of the movement. Because of the major role played by race in America, African American women were those most often sidelined by suffrage organizations.

The *New York Tribune* captured the issue in a March 1913 cartoon titled "Just like the men!" The drawing depicts a White woman holding up her hand to stop a Black suffragist from joining her. Both their signs read "Votes for Women." The caption reads "Votes for WHITE women."[69]

Of the two most prominent suffrage organizations, NAWSA was slightly more liberal on race than the "radical" NWP. This was evident, as the cartoon attests, in the organizing of the 1913 National Parade in D.C. Lead organizer Alice Paul tried to keep Black women out of the massive march, while the NAWSA leadership countermanded her.

Paul was hyper-focused on winning a federal suffrage amendment at all costs, and race was a divisive issue. Her thinking: to achieve suffrage for all women, votes of southern politicians were needed. If Black women appeared in the parade, White southern women might not participate. And the appearance of mixing races at a public event could upset potential supporters. Paul was willing to bar Black women for the "greater good." Race was not the issue, only suffrage.

NAWSA had, in earlier years, blocked Black women from conventions in the South and rejected "racial issues" as its concern. But in 1906, NAWSA affirmed that it would "not advocate exclusion of race or class" in its pursuit of suffrage. In 1913, whatever individual members or clubs thought, NAWSA did not want to bar any women from the first national suffrage parade.

NAWSA ordered Paul to allow Black women to march in the parade. Begrudgingly, Alice Paul acceded to the directions—but informed "colored" women that they must come and speak with her first. And in the plan of march, she placed Black women at the end of the parade.[70]

At the last minute, NAWSA still attempted to rein back Paul's determined segregation of marchers. Three days before the event, they sent this night telegram: "Am informed that Parade committee has so strongly urged Colored women not to march that it amounts to official discrimination which is distinctly contrary to instructions from National headquarters. Please instruct all marshals to see that all colored women who wish to march shall be accorded every service given to other marchers."[71]

A few years later, after breaking with NAWSA, Alice Paul's NWP continued to limit participation of Black women. Paul also used the divisiveness of American race relations to solicit southern support. When campaigning in the South, for instance, organizers used stories of forced integration of White women with Black women in jail to show how wickedly they were treated.

NWP historian Inez H. Irwin wrote that jail officials "put colored prisoners to sleep in the same room with the Suffragists…[and] set the Suffragists to paint the lavatories used by the colored women." She made little reference to the non-suffragist White women in jail with them. After describing being forced to share quarters with Black women, she noted this: "Our thoughts turn to the outside world. Will the women care? Will enough women believe that through such humiliation all may win freedom?"

And later, in the South, Irwin wrote:

> *The speakers had extraordinary experiences, especially those who went into the strongholds of the Democrats in the South. Again and again when they told about the jail conditions, and how white women were forced into association with the colored prisoners, were even compelled to paint the toilets used by the colored prisoners, men would rise in the audience and say, "There are a score of men here who'll go right up to Washington and burn that jail down." It has been said that Warden Zinkham [sic] received by mail so many threats against his life that he went armed.*[72]

Racist opposition to suffrage was quite strong. Some senators spoke openly of opposing suffrage solely to prevent more Black people from trying to vote. At the NWP, Irwin even noted complaints to them "that 5 little colored girls marched in a suffrage parade in Columbus OH."[73] While Paul did maintain communication with several Black suffrage leaders, the only Black people regularly at the NWP headquarters were servers in the tearoom and the janitor and helper who brought hot bricks to keep picketers' feet warm in winter.

Yet multiple anti-racist efforts involving both Black and White leaders also existed at the same time. The Federal Council of Churches, for instance, called for the country to address civil rights of "colored persons": equal wages for equal work, equal or at least adequate schools, adequate housing, police protection and equality before the law.[74] And a federal anti-lynching bill was proposed in 1918—although, after a prolonged fight, the bill was defeated by filibuster in 1922.

Before the 1921 NWP conference, an estimated sixty representatives from twenty Black women's groups met with Alice Paul. They requested support in battling Jim Crow laws that already prevented Black men from voting and would do the same to women. But Paul said no to this "race" problem.

Some NWP members, however, did not believe in this distinction between racism and feminism. They picketed for suffrage while also pushing the NWP to do more for Black women. White allies included Mary White Ovington and Harriot Stanton Blatch. They urged the NWP leadership to publicly address the problem of Black women's disenfranchisement, to no avail. Their request for inclusion of a Black suffragist as a speaker at the 1921 conference was turned down, although the all-White Daughters of the American Revolution was granted time.[75]

At the conference itself, Ella Murray urged the NWP to promote legislation for strict enforcement of the Nineteenth Amendment.[76] The response was the same: no.

Even earlier, in 1913, New England attorney Lucy Daniels wrote to Paul and the organizers of the national suffrage parade in D.C. She included fifty dollars to induce the Parade Committee to recruit one hundred "Negro women" to participate. Perhaps they could contact local churches or Dr. W.E.B. DuBois to assist?

The money was returned: the parade was nothing to do with "churches, sects, political parties, race or color." Daniels's response: since "Negroes" had reason to fear their welcome, the organizers could put effort into recruiting them just as they were already doing with White women.[77]

In the years after the 1921 conference, the long struggle for voting access continued without the NWP. Elizabeth helped organize the 1921 conference. She understood how race was used by the NWP but never mentioned any concern about treatment of Black women.

AN EXCEPTION TO THE RULE

One Black woman and NWP member who maintained positive relations with Alice Paul was Mary Church Terrell. A confident leader herself, Terrell was highly educated, well traveled and a prominent figure in D.C.

Terrell was born in 1863 in Tennessee, where her formerly enslaved parents established a financially successful life. And as with Elizabeth's family, Terrell's parents—especially her mother— were determined their daughter get an education. They sent her north to get it.

Terrell graduated from Ohio's Oberlin College, integrated and coeducational. After teaching and then traveling overseas, she married and settled in D.C. Her leadership skills and commitment to social activism carried her through the rest of her life. She battled racism and sexism while promoting world peace, education and equality for all.

Mary Church Terrell. Date unknown. *Library of Congress.*

Through Terrell's willingness to attend and speak at meetings, she knew NAWSA's leadership well. She became a conduit between the African American community and the White suffrage community. And when Paul established the NWP, Terrell also maintained that connection. She was not the only Black member of either organization but was one of the most important.

In addition to suffrage and education, Terrell also helped start and worked with the National Association of Colored Women, D.C.'s Women Wage Earners Association (restaurant, hotel and domestic workers), the International Women's Congress—the list goes on. And in her eighties, she initiated a legal battle that resulted in the 1953 reintegration of restaurants in D.C.

Terrell did all this while writing and publishing streams of articles, raising two daughters and suffering the physical and emotional effects of miscarriage. Her health is important because, too often, strong female leaders are dismissed as simply "tough" or "unfeeling." That image can hide the reality of struggles, even apart from facing any sexism and/or racism.

From Paul's perspective, Terrell was everything she wanted in an NWP supporter: highly respected, well educated, a gifted orator and respectful of Paul's leadership. And this relationship was an opportunity to maintain communications with educated Black women in the District and across the country. The only "problem" was Terrell's race, given the NWP's efforts to appease southern supporters and politicians on this issue.

Terrell understood politicking around race—certainly better than the NWP, because she lived with it. She looked past the exclusionary aspects of the NWP because she believed in the end goal: women's suffrage. And at the same time, she continued pushing Paul to work on voting rights for all women, not just Whites. Like Paul, Terrell played the long game.

After Paul brutally rejected Black women's request for support in 1921, Terrell merely noted: "Alice Paul had displayed the most painful lack of tact I had ever seen."[78] Terrell went right on with her life's work: lifting people up—and working with Paul when she shared the same goal.

Chapter 6

LIMITS OF AN EYEWITNESS

An eyewitness account, such as Elizabeth's, can both illuminate and obfuscate. Such testimony provides a powerful sense of time and place. But memories fail, audience affects language and preconceived expectations shape reality. Elizabeth was writing down events as they happened, providing an immediacy and detail that might be lost in memory. But she also brought a viewpoint shaped by privilege.

RACE

When she was born in 1896, Elizabeth's greatest privilege was being "White." This gave her access to certain school and work options unavailable to other people. And she could choose to see—or not—civil rights problems around her.

Race was a defining element of Texas life when Elizabeth's family arrived from Ohio to start peach farming about 1909. The major groups were White, Black and Native American. Hispanic people, primarily Mexican Americans at the time, were considered "White" in the Census. But they were often segregated and, in Texas, were subjected to lynching and other violence.

Elizabeth's high school was for White students only, severely limiting her Black neighbors' access to education. She was in the first class of Rice

Institute (now University), created explicitly as both coeducational and all White. The school did not integrate until 1964.

The farming community was also divided by race—not physically, but in public services and social acceptance. Violence was common. When Elizabeth was fourteen, a nearby rural area had a White-on-Black massacre of local farmers. Despite testimony from the sheriff and multiple arrests, no one was ever brought to trial.[79]

Family Support

Another of Elizabeth's great assets was family modeling and support. One grandmother was a suffragist and a leader in a national Union veterans' auxiliary. Her mother was a businesswoman and activist. An only child, Elizabeth bore the full force of her parents' interest, support and expectations of success.

While Elizabeth deprecated her own speaking ability, she attended and was encouraged to participate in farm association meetings with her mother. This practice likely helped when she entered and won a Carnegie Peace Oratory Contest in college.

Income and Class

Financially, Elizabeth was born into a dual-income, middle-class life. Her mother, who established a successful stenography business, was part of an emerging force of primarily White female professionals. Stenography developed quickly in the late 1800s, paying well for recording business, government and legal proceedings.

In Ohio, Elizabeth's parents probably suffered reversals during the devastating depression of the 1890s. Fewer contracts for her mother and less work for her father could have wiped out their income, even as the family expanded to include Elizabeth. Both parents had family in the area, which could have helped with shared housing.

Their situation likely qualified them for short-term government relief, although whether they received it is unknown. They were "deserving," under government rules, because they could prove they had been working and were now "non-employed." This set them apart from just "an ordinary cause of poverty." This dual relief structure kept natural allies—all those struggling with little income—apart and limited the burden on the government. Reflecting a broadly held societal view, "paupers" were undeserving and probably lazy, while "workingmen" were decent and just couldn't find jobs.

This requirement to prove prior employment fell hard on poor Black southerners moving north to get work. With few schools available to non-White students in the South, literacy rates were low. Non-Whites had little reason to carry papers proving details of prior jobs, especially if they were unskilled laborers.

Government relief funds also required that recipients be "qualified" to obtain citizenship even if they were not currently citizens. At the time, federal law barred non-White immigrants from obtaining citizenship. So first-generation Asians could not receive assistance. And native-born Asian Americans suffered a similar problem to African Americans: how to prove employment in low-paying, little-documented jobs.[80]

In Elizabeth's case, her parents got through the depression and created a new life in Texas.

Political Access

When Elizabeth was arrested in 1919, her mother immediately telegrammed Senator Sheppard of Texas, requesting him to visit the jail. Sheppard was a supporter of and good friend to suffrage.

The senator did not visit the jail personally but asked the superintendent of police for a report. "I agree with you," he noted to Elizabeth's mother, "that the only effective thing that can be done to cure the situation [of women arrested for picketing] is to pass the Susan B. Anthony Amendment."[81]

The police referred the matter of jail conditions to the D.C. Board of Charities, which noted its frustration:

> *You understand, of course, that the representatives of the Women's National Party that have been confined in the Jail and Workhouse at various times during the past few years have been a source of very great annoyance. We have endeavored to make conditions as good as possible; but it seems to be a fact that these women are better satisfied when they*

*can find conditions about which to complain than otherwise. They have
no regard for discipline and have resorted to every conceivable method to
disorganize our institutions and excite comment and publicity.*

So the telegram to Senator Sheppard did not affect the outcome of
Elizabeth's arrest but did provoke a response.

Chapter 7

OTHER VIEWPOINTS

In the United States there is an imperative need of meddlers today—active, insistent and fearless meddlers who will spend their time investigating institutions, customs and laws whose effect upon the citizens of any color or class is depressing or bad....Meddlers, more meddlers let us have....Those who dare ask prejudiced, caste-ridden bigots by what right they humiliate and harass their fellowmen simply on account of a difference in color, class or races.[82]
—Mary Church Terrell, 1905

Memories and history are shaped by images. But while suffrage pictures usually feature White women, leaders and workers across the country were more diverse. Some have been acknowledged and honored; others disappeared from sight.[83]

History lessons also often focus on "heroes" as mythically perfect people that led the fight for justice. But people are not carved and polished figures. They are flesh and blood and contradictions. They are still heroes—just not perfect.

These are selected figures—there are many, many more—who faced challenges due to race, legal barriers and/or social status. They were no more perfect than anyone else, but they fought to make a difference in society. And while many were leaders in their fields, behind them were similar women who, like Elizabeth, kept the movement going forward.

Suffragists were organized in every state and territory. Do you know the stories of those who supported suffrage in your community?

AFRICAN AMERICAN

As discussed above, African American people faced particularly difficult barriers when working in suffrage. Yet many found ways to speak out and participate.

ANNA JULIA COOPER was an activist and teacher in Washington, D.C. In her book, *A Voice from the South*, she writes:

> *The cause of freedom is not the cause of a race or a sect, a party or a class, it is the cause of human kind, the very birthright of humanity....And* [for suffrage] *specially important is it that there be no confusion of ideas among its leaders as to its scope and universality....It is not the intelligent woman vs. the ignorant woman; nor the white woman vs. the black, the brown, and the red, it is not even the cause of woman vs. man. Nay, 'tis woman's strongest vindication for speaking that the world needs to hear her voice. It would be subversive of every human interest that the cry of one-half the human family be stifled. Woman in stepping from the pedestal of statue-like inactivity in the domestic shrine, and daring to think and move and speak, to undertake to help shape, mold, and direct the thought of her age, is merely completing the circle of the world's vision.*[84]

MARY BURNETT TALBERT was an educator, writer and activist. Like Mary Church Terrell, Talbert spent most of her life fighting for Black women and equality for all. She first gained fame for organizing protests against racist depictions of Black people used at the 1901 Pan American Expo. She worked in social justice, served as president of the National Association of Colored Women's Clubs and was involved with many other groups.

NELLIE QUANDER was an educator, civic leader and first national president of the Alpha Kappa Alpha sorority. Quander ensured participation of Howard University students in the 1913 National Suffrage Parade in D.C.

NATIVE AMERICAN

Indigenous American people played a complex role in women's suffrage. They had limited voting rights and none on reservations. Suffrage orators sometimes used the "ignorant savage" image to contrast them with the intelligent White woman—both unable to vote. And East Coast White

Anna J. Cooper. 1901. *Library of Congress.*

women had a different perspective than those in the West, still fighting to obtain and keep land.

Yet early suffragists such as Matilda Joslyn Gage and Elizabeth Cady Stanton also pointed to the Iroquois women in New England as models of political participation. Native American women had a voice in selecting leaders and control of their own property, in sharp contrast to the suffragists. And White women led a national petition drive to stop the 1830 Indian Removal Act.[85] That ultimately unsuccessful effort was an early example of women uniting for political change.

But when did the "Indian" people speak for themselves? Rarely. In suffrage, the exceptions were well-educated Native Americans often caught between different societies. To have their voices heard, they had to conform to the lives of the middle- and upper-class White women who were the majority of the movement.

By 1913's national suffrage parade, the "noble savage" image was deeply embedded in American society. A picture from the event shows a woman and young boy or girl in Native American clothes on horses. But

SAVAGERY TO "CIVILIZATION"

THE INDIAN WOMEN: We whom you pity as drudges reached centuries ago the goal that you are now nearing

This drawing captured the suffragists' belief in Native American women's greater civic rights. Joseph (Udo) Keppler Jr., artist. *Puck* magazine, 1914. *Library of Congress.*

Zitkala-Ša (Gertrude Simmons Bonnin). Joseph T. Keiley, artist. 1898. *National Portrait Gallery, Smithsonian Institute.*

are they Native American people? Or are they White people dressed up as part of the homage to the Indians?

Organizers reported that future representative Jeannette Rankin of Montana was "expect[ed] to get a very handsome girl to take the part of the famous Indian pioneer," Sacajawea. But the organizers canceled a float titled "The Primitive American Woman With a Voice in Tribal Government." So while newspaper reports said a "real" American Indian rode on a float, that may not be true.

Marie Louise Bottineau Baldwin (Turtle Mountain Chippewa) was a lawyer and activist who marched in the parade. While organizers wanted a float with a romantic tribute to Native American women, she chose to march as a modern Indigenous woman with fellow lawyers and suffragists.[86] She noted in 1914: "The trouble in this Indian question which I meet again and again is that it is not the Indian who needs to be educated so constantly up to the white man, but that the white man needs to be educated to the Indian."[87]

Zitkala-Ša, Gertrude Simmons Bonnin (Yankton Dakota, Sioux), was a musician, composer, writer and activist. Probably the most prominent Native American suffragist, Zitkala-Ša spoke at the NWP headquarters in 1918 and at the 1921 conference. She believed that Native Americans could be citizens of both the United States and of their tribes.

Yet despite inviting Zitkala-Ša to speak, the NWP said no to pursuing suffrage for Native Americans. As with Black women's request for help with voting, the NWP did not see Native American suffrage as a woman's issue. On the other hand, the General Federation of Women's Clubs hired Zitkala-Ša as both a speaker and an investigator of Native American conditions.

Laura Cornelius Kellogg (Wisconsin Oneida) was a writer, community planner and activist. In a 1915 interview featured in the *Washington Herald*, she said: "We (Native American) women have always had equal civil powers with the men. And it is a cause of astonishment to us that you white women are only now, in this twentieth century, claiming what has been the Indian woman's privilege as far back as history traces."[88]

Asian Women

The role of Asian American women in the suffrage fight was limited by their small population in the United States at the time. The first major wave of Chinese in the West came to work on building railroads. As the need for laborers decreased, however, the U.S. enacted laws to limit their population. The 1875 Page Act banned Asian "unfree" laborers and women destined for "immoral purposes." But in application, the act was used to exclude almost all female Chinese immigrants.

The 1882 Chinese Exclusion Act went much further. Chinese laborers, both "skilled and unskilled," were barred from further entry to the United States. These restrictions exempted some Chinese, including professors and college students. But none were eligible for citizenship.

The occasional special treatment of educated Chinese was also evident in the suffrage movement. In 1912, for instance, rumors flew that the new regime in China might grant women the vote. NAWSA used this as an opportunity to raise Chinese visibility, to emphasize that another country was ahead of the United States in recognizing women's suffrage. Mabel Lee (see below) was asked to ride at the head of a New York suffrage parade in 1912. And the organizers of the 1913 national parade arranged housing for four Chinese women.

MABEL PING-HUA LEE (China) was an economist, activist and church leader. Lee arrived in the United States at a young age, to join her missionary father in New York's Chinatown. She was educated at a U.S. high school and Barnard College but, as a Chinese immigrant, could not become a citizen.

Yet Lee was a suffragist from a young age. In her teens, she recruited Chinese women to participate in the massive 1912 New York suffrage parade, riding proudly at the front. She gave speeches and wrote about suffrage and civil rights at college. And Lee was known for her speech "China's Submerged Half," which advocated for both suffrage and women's civic participation.

KANG TUNG PIH/KANG TONGBI (China) was a writer and activist. Like Lee, Kang

CHINESE GIRL WANTS VOTE

Miss Lee Ready to Enter Barnard, to Ride in Suffrage Parade.

Mabel Ping-Hua Lee. *New-York Endowment Tribune*. April 1912. *Library of Congress.*

attended Barnard College. She was a member of the class of 1909. (In contrast, the college did not admit an African American student until Zora Neale Hurston in 1925.) Kang was the daughter of a prominent Chinese reformer. At college, Kang joined the Collegiate Equal Suffrage League. She said, "When I finish here, I am going back to China to wake up my countrywomen. I am deeply interested in suffrage, and hope to arouse the women of China to a realization of their rights."[89]

KOMAKO KIMURA (Japan) was an actress, writer and activist. In 1917, the famed actress was in New York and marched in a suffrage parade. She garnered great attention, combining traditional Japanese dress and makeup with a "Woman Suffrage Party" sash. A radical in her homeland, Komako visited the United States in part to learn more about suffrage and to raise money for her work in Japan on women's civil rights.

HISPANIC AMERICANS

The Hispanic/Latino population in the United States was relatively small for most of the suffrage years. But as western territories joined the Union, more Hispanic women fought for and gained the vote. And as in other groups, class and race often defined lives and activism.[90]

AURORA LUCERO-WHITE LEA was a writer, educator, folklorist and activist. Lucero was from a prominent political family in New Mexico. Beginning in high school, she was a passionate advocate for respecting the Spanish speakers of America. This included insisting on suffrage materials in both Spanish and English. She and Adelina Otero-Warren spoke at a Congressional Union for Woman Suffrage event in Santa Fe in 1915.

ADELINA "NINA" OTERO-WARREN was an educator, agency director, politician and real estate agent. The "brainy one," according to her family, Otero-Warren began working with the Congressional Union for Woman Suffrage in 1914. She became head of the New Mexico chapter and led lobbying efforts for both state and federal suffrage. In 1920, the state ratified the Nineteenth Amendment. The following year, an amendment to the state constitution allowed women to run for any political office. Otero-Warren was the Republican candidate for New Mexico's sole House seat in 1922 but lost the election.

MARIA GUADALUPE EVANGELINA DE LOPEZ was an educator, translator and activist. A Californian, Lopez worked as a teacher and translator and,

Adelina "Nina" Otero-Warren. 1923.
Library of Congress.

in World War I, as an ambulance driver in France. From a young age, she devoted herself to promoting equal rights, including suffrage. Lopez translated materials and did extensive speaking and outreach to include Spanish-speaking Californians in the effort to gain women the vote.

U.S. Territories

Residents of the District of Columbia, as noted earlier, had no voice in politics. That was equally true for territories of the United States. Yet District residents fought for suffrage, both federal and their own representation. Women in U.S. territories, too, organized and protested their lack of suffrage.

Hawaii

Women in the Kingdom of Hawaii traditionally had power in government through lines of nobility. With the takeover of Hawaii by the United States, however, their roles were significantly diminished. The act establishing the Hawaiian Territory specifically aligned voting rights with those provided by the United States Constitution.

Hawaiians became U.S. citizens under the act. But as a territory, Hawaii had no representation in Congress and no votes in federal elections. The local legislature was elected by Hawaiian men only.

As with the federal campaign for suffrage, little movement was evident until the 1910s. Then, as on the mainland, more women began to organize and push again for their rights. Carrie Chapman Catt, at that time president of the International Woman Suffrage Alliance, made an inspiring visit in 1912.

Wilhelmine Kekelaokalaninui Widemann Dowsett was a Hawaiian social and civic leader. Dowsett worked from the beginning of the territorial establishment to ensure women had a voice. She was descended on her mother's side from Hawaiian nobility and married to a successful White Hawaiian businessman and politician. In 1912, she boosted the local effort by creating the Women's Equal Suffrage Association of Hawaii. Members were primarily Native or biracial women. Initially, White women appeared less interested in working to increase Native votes, although some participated. By 1919, however, many more women were ready to join their mainland peers in working for suffrage.

With a bill from President Wilson giving Hawaii the choice of suffrage approval, the time appeared set. Dowsett and other suffragists gathered as the Hawaiian senate passed the bill. Dowsett made clear that this was suffrage for all Hawaiian women: Native, White and Asian.

Unfortunately, the Hawaiian house of representatives balked. They wanted the (male) electorate to vote on it the following year. Frustrated but determined, suffragists combined lobbying the U.S. Congress with outreach to prepare women for potential victory. And on August 26, 1920, Hawaiian women won the vote along with their mainland sisters—except they had no federal representation. That would come with statehood in 1959.

Emma ʻAʻima Aʻii Nāwahī was a politician, community leader and publisher. Nāwahī was the daughter of a Native Hawaiian mother and a Chinese father. Her husband was a politician, and she became a confidante of Queen Liliʻuokalani. When the monarchy was overthrown, Nāwahī worked to oppose the annexation of the country by the United States. She helped establish the Democratic Party of Hawaii, also opposed to annexation. And in the 1910s, she supported the efforts of suffragists in Hawaii to attain the vote.

PUERTO RICO

In 1917, after the United States took over the island, Puerto Rican citizens became U.S. citizens. But this came with no voting rights, even after the Nineteenth Amendment passed in 1920. Only states of America had that privilege. Within Puerto Rico's territorial political system, only men had the vote. But calls for suffrage had started many years before.

ANA ROQUE DE DUPREY was a magazine publisher and educator. Duprey began advocating for suffrage and women's education in the late 1800s. After the change in government, Duprey increased her efforts and founded the Puerto Rican Feminist League. Repeatedly, bills were presented to the legislature but failed to pass.

LUISA CAPETILLO was a writer, social activist, factory worker and union leader. Capetillo worked her way up in factory jobs to become a *lectora*—a reader who entertained the cigar makers as they worked. To inspire them, she read politics, fiction, historical narratives and other stimulating writings. As a suffragist, she believed in universal access to voting and was against proposed literacy tests. Her union endorsed women's suffrage, education and legal rights.

In 1926, Puerto Rican advocates for universal suffrage met with National Woman's Party representatives. They asked for help in requesting the United States Congress to extend women's suffrage to Puerto Rico. In response to this external pressure, in 1929, Puerto Rican suffrage passed—but only for literate women. After years of further campaigning, full suffrage was won in 1935.

PEOPLE WITH DISABILITIES

The term *disabilities* covers a vast number of conditions, many not obvious to onlookers. Some suffragists did have known challenges, and a few are mentioned here. Others may today have identified as having medical conditions or disabilities. At the time, however, medical science and public discourse tended to characterize differences negatively.

Some struggles also were more acceptable than others. Physical challenges, when "overcome," were often accepted. But suffrage groups, feeding into public stereotyping, often contrasted educated women with other disenfranchised people: "idiots" and "the insane," as well as "Indians" and "convicts."

Harriet Tubman. 1911. *Library of Congress.*

HARRIET TUBMAN was a public speaker, activist and guide on the Underground Railroad. After fleeing slavery herself, Tubman guided other enslaved people to freedom. She spent decades touring the country promoting equal rights and women's suffrage. While still enslaved, according to her account, an iron weight was thrown at a fleeing enslaved youth. The projectile missed and hit twelve-year-old Harriet's head instead. She received no medical care. For the rest of her long life, Tubman suffered from severe headaches, seizures and other crippling effects—symptoms that seem to align with epilepsy. She spoke openly of her physical disabilities and continued to work for others' freedom and equality.

HELEN KELLER was a writer and activist. Keller was the most prominent identified woman with disabilities advocating for suffrage. Her major interest, however, was the larger picture of economic and political inequalities. A member of the Congressional Union Advisory Council, she wrote this in 1916 about the creation of the National Woman's Party (the "New Women's Party," in her words):

> *Now we believe that it takes both men and women to run the world and run it right. The New Woman's Party is an expression of this idea, but until political equality is secured, we must put women's interests first. The same wiseacres who argue against women's suffrage argued against higher education for women 60 years ago. They solemnly asserted that education would unfit women to be wives and mothers, and they hinted at the possible extermination of the race.*
>
> *They insisted that the majority of women were content with their lot in life. Only a few strong-minded women wanted to go to college. Today, they declare that women do not really want the vote; that only a few mannish women are clamoring for suffrage. Such arguments are always used to resist the march of progress.*[91]

Despite passage of the Nineteenth Amendment, however, many barriers remained for people with disabilities. In response to long and active lobbying by disability groups, federal laws now require greater accessibility. These laws, particularly addressing physical barriers, heavily rely on local and state action.

PERSONAL IDENTIFIERS

During the events described in this book, a person's gender identity and sexuality were assumed and rarely discussed. Our contemporary understanding of and language for these aspects of life did not exist. Most women identified simply as either single or married.

This does not mean, however, that people were not living outside these rigid self-identifiers. But the forced discretion of the time silenced many women, leaving little trace of their thoughts on life, gender and sex. And others who did live publicly in "radical" ways have been left out of historical accounts.

Recent scholarship has created greater understanding of how personal identities and relationships impacted lives and work. By studying letters, journals and personal narratives, some history has become fuller and clearer. But much remains unknown due to limited primary source material.

DR. MARIE EQUI, MD, was a doctor and activist. Born in Massachusetts in 1872, Equi dropped out of high school to work and support her family. Several years later, she moved with a woman friend to Oregon. Equi eventually went to medical school and started practicing in 1903, becoming a beloved "Doc" to generations of working-class patients. Politically, Equi was a progressive. She worked on state suffrage, provided birth control to her patients and sought improved working conditions.

But in 1913, the violent treatment of striking workers radicalized her, and she declared herself an anarchist. Arrested for opposing World War I—although only with words—when appeals were finished, she served ten months in prison after the war was over. Equi lived openly in romantic same-sex relationships. The prison sentence, she believed, was a reflection of homophobia.[92]

The following are a few women who might identify differently today.

ALICE DUNBAR-NELSON was a writer, poet, teacher and organizer. Dunbar-Nelson encompassed many roles in her life. And always, she focused on challenging people to do more and better. For suffrage, she went on speaking tours in Delaware and Pennsylvania. During ratification, she often shared a stage with Mary Church Terrell. And as diaries and letters revealed after her passing, she had loving relationships with men and women.[93]

DR. MARGARET JESSIE CHUNG was a doctor, civic leader and activist. The first Chinese American woman to become a physician, Chung devoted her life to serving others. As a doctor, she served both Chinatown and Hollywood. And she did so in her own distinctive style, sometimes in men's clothes and sometimes called Mike—that is, when she wasn't called Mom. Starting with the Sino-Japanese War in 1937 and through World War II, she created a network of service member "adopted sons." Even after California women won the right to vote, Chung continued advocating for all American women to have equal access. Chung apparently had relationships with other women.[94]

Religion

In 1906, the vast majority of Americans identified as Christian—though they were not necessarily part of any church. Protestants dominated, with Catholics a distant second but rapidly increasing population. Jewish congregations were a small fraction of these numbers.[95]

But the numbers were very different in microcosms such as New York. That population, surging with European immigrants, was closer to one-third Jewish and one-third Catholic residents. And those immigrants included many interested in equal rights and suffrage.

The Religious Society of Friends, or Quakers, was particularly well represented, especially in early leadership of the suffrage movement. Their faith community provided them with experience in public speaking, organizing and negotiating.

By the late 1800s, Protestant women of diverse denominations were well represented in local and national suffrage organizations. But women of other religions also participated, in both leadership and membership. For D.C.'s 1913 national parade, a Maryland committee organizer noted their inclusiveness: an Italian Catholic woman and a Jewish woman with a Yiddish banner would both be participating. Catholic representation was important, as the Church itself was opposed to suffrage. And while Jewish women participated in suffrage, the National Council of Jewish Women never endorsed it.

Social activist Lucy Burns, an Irish American Catholic from the Bronx, was cofounder of what became the National Woman's Party. Brilliant at school, she went on to advanced studies in Berlin and at Oxford. But suffrage in England became her cause, and she spent several years with the militant suffragettes. She met Alice Paul there, and they bonded over frustration with the United States' lack of suffrage. Together, they created the Congressional

Lucy Burns. 1916. *Library of Congress.*

Union for Woman Suffrage and the National Woman's Party. While Paul was a visionary, Burns was a passionate and pragmatic leader: organizing, speaking, implementing and withstanding the Night of Horrors with steely determination.[96]

SELINA SOLOMONS was a social activist and writer. An ardent suffragist, middle-class and a Sephardic Jew, Solomons worked with Maud Younger and others in California to win state suffrage. Seeing working-class women left out of suffrage efforts by elites, she founded the Votes for Women Club specifically for them.

On election night in 1911, with a California suffrage amendment on the ballot, supporters were in despair. Early returns that Tuesday showed the probable defeat of their amendment. Even San Francisco, where Solomons and others were based, apparently voted against it. As she reported later:

At Election Committee headquarters all was gloom. Determined to put a good face on defeat, next day, we dressed in our best, including badges and regalia….The latest edition of the Bulletin, *one of our strongest supporters, had declared our defeat by eight thousand votes. But after a second sorrowing night—"that 'speck' of light!"*

Returns slowly coming in from remote country districts…had nearly done away with the adverse majority. Even the city kept showing up better; less than two to one against….Never did the phrase, "another county heard from" seem fraught with such happy meaning!…It had been Black Wednesday indeed, when we peered through darkness. Now today seemed Holy Thursday, as the majority in our favor crept slowly up, from a few hundred votes to three thousand and more!…

We had kept back our womanish tears on that Black Wednesday. Now we gave free rein to our emotions, in both manly and womanly fashion, with handshaking and back slapping as well as hugging and kissing one another. The women in the street looked just about the same as ever. We wondered how they could![97]

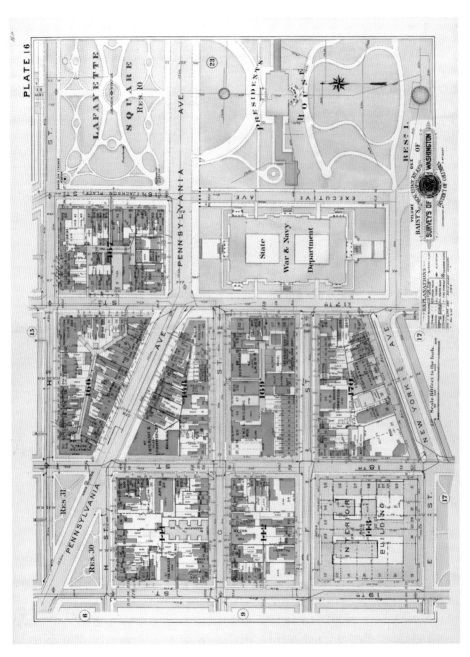

A 1919 map with White House and Lafayette Square. Baist's Real Estate Surveys of Washington, D.C. *Library of Congress.*

Appendix

SITES OF INTEREST

Headquarter Locations: Congressional Union and NWP

1913–1916: 1420 F Street NW
Harris & Ewing Photographers, who documented much of the NWP activities, was at 1313 F Street NW.

1916–1917: 21 Madison Place (Cameron House), Lafayette Square

1918–1921: 14 Jackson Place, Lafayette Square
This block of houses has been replaced by Federal-style buildings. The location is now 722 Jackson Place.

Circa 1921–1929: 21–25 First Street NE, Capitol Hill
Known as the "Old Brick Capitol," sold for redevelopment.

1929–2016: 144 Constitutional Avenue NE
Donated to the National Park Service and now the Belmont-Paul Women's Equality National Monument. Operates as a museum.

OTHER SITES

Demonstration and picketing locations:
　　Lafayette Square, Lafayette Statue
　　U.S. Capitol
　　Russell Senate Office Building
　　The White House

National American Woman Suffrage Association (NAWSA) Headquarters
　　1626 Rhode Island Avenue NW

NOTES

Chapter 1

1. Elizabeth went by many names over the years. Born Hildegard Elizabeth Kalb, she dropped Hildegard in college. Around 1922, she dropped Kalb and began using her mother's maiden name, Green. In 1934, she married and became Elizabeth Handy—except in some of her writing, where she remained Elizabeth Green.
2. Letter quoted in Kimberly A. Hamlin, "Fallen Women Who Won the Vote," *Humanities*, April 13, 2020, https://www.neh.gov/article/fallen-woman-who-won-vote. To understand the NAWSA's "soft" lobbying and one of its campaigners, see Hamlin's *Free Thinker: Sex, Suffrage and the Extraordinary Life of Helen Hamilton Gardener* (New York: W.W. Norton, 2020).
3. This idea that men would not use the same tactics on Black women as Black men was not true. Violent voter suppression simply expanded to include enfranchised Black women.
4. Inez Haynes Irwin, *The Story of the Woman's Party* (New York: Harcourt, Brace, 1921), available from Project Gutenberg.
5. Detailed NWP timelines are available on websites such as those of the Library of Congress and the Alice Paul Institute and the University of Washington's *Mapping American Social Movements* Project. For suffrage timelines, see Crusade for the Vote, the University of Rochester's Susan B. Anthony Center and the National Park Service's "*US Women's Suffrage Timeline*."
6. *Suffragette* was used as a pejorative term. Militant British suffragists embraced the word, but suffragists in the United States did not. When World War I began in 1914, moderate and radical wings of the British suffrage movement shifted their focus to war work. In 1918, as part of a bill to eliminate property requirements

for male voters, women gained the vote if they were over thirty years old and met property requirements. Finally, in 1928, they won full enfranchisement.

7. The Library of Congress has records from NAWSA and NWP. In addition, it holds the Harris & Ewing photography collection, including images of many NWP people and events.

8. See Benjamin Alexander, *Coxey's Army: Popular Protest in the Gilded Age* (Baltimore: Johns Hopkins University Press, 2015).

9. *Washington Herald*, October 23, 1918. The NWP was careful to not criticize the war or the soldiers. They also used the president's own words as material. Public cries of "sedition" arose, however, when they implied that Germany was more of a democracy than the United States.

10. The *San Antonio Express* published the story on October 1, 1918.

11. For personal accounts of that night, see Doris Stevens, *Jailed for Freedom* (New York: Boni and Liveright, 1920), available from Project Gutenberg.

12. The D.C. Court of Appeals ruled in 1918 that the arrests and subsequent imprisonments were illegal. Six suffragists sued for damages, but dropped the case in January 1920.

13. Elizabeth was much younger than most at NWP headquarters. Most people she mentions are in their late twenties to late forties.

Chapter 2

14. From Oregon, three Wold sisters participated in NWP activities: Clara, Emma and Cora.

15. A cornerstone of today's naturopathy, Henry Lindlahr's *Nature Cure* emphasized a diet of vegetables and fruits, fresh air and exercise. Elizabeth's mother was a patient and working at Lindlahr's health center outside Chicago. Elizabeth worked there the summer before arriving in D.C.

16. A quick dig at the venerable NAWSA, under the leadership of Carrie Chapman Catt.

17. The "quality" was both deliberate and a natural result of using volunteers. Deliberate because Alice Paul recruited "respectable," primarily White women who, if attacked, presented the greatest shock value in publicity. Natural because women with the confidence, time and money to face public abuse and possible jail time were few. Many women repeatedly arrested were NWP employees. Paychecks helped them to live independent of their families.

18. A Democrat, Dr. Ellis was a University of Texas professor and heavily involved with suffrage work in Texas.

19. Elizabeth was in the first class of the new Rice Institute (now Rice University), graduating in 1916. In the Carnegie Peace Oratory Contest, she won first place at state and second in regional.

20. Cunningham was head of the Texas Equal Suffrage Association. She devoted years to both state and federal campaigns with NAWSA. Her expertise included building partnerships and persuading politicians.
21. Maud Powell Jamison of Norfolk, Virginia, was a teacher who started in local suffrage work and then moved on to the federal fight. She was with the first group of NWP picketers in January 1917, was repeatedly jailed and still kept working.
22. Elizabeth was quoting the very charge leveled against the NWP for its work.
23. At that time, Sinn Féin was struggling for political power and Irish self-determination. Elizabeth's original negative views were undoubtedly influenced by a widespread American Protestant dislike of the Irish "race," based on their Catholicism, commitment to their homeland and purported wild behavior. The American media generally favored the British side.
24. Elizabeth used *séance* to mean "session" or "meeting."
25. Reed Smoot, R-UT. As a prominent leader in the LDS (Mormon) Church, his election in 1903 was a source of controversy. Key Pittman, D-NV, served from 1913 until his death in 1940.
26. Hazel Hunkins, NWP member and organizer from Montana, participated in picketing the White House and served time in jail several times. She had a degree in chemistry but was unable to find work in that field due to her sex. She later moved to the UK, worked as a correspondent and campaigned for equal rights.
27. Benet was in office only briefly. He filled the seat of Senator Tillman, who had died in July 1918.
28. "His peculiar situation" being that he had consistently opposed efforts for federal suffrage until very recently.
29. Elizabeth was using medical practices she had learned at the Lindlahr Institute. The trunk pack is a cold, wet cloth compress of layered muslin or toweling wrapped around the torso, under the armpits, then covered with a dry wrap of flannel or wool.
30. Edith R. Ainge, "Aingy," was a great source of comfort to Elizabeth and others. She had done suffrage work in New York before joining the picketers at NWP HQ in 1917. Arrested at least five times, she was part of the group that suffered abuse in the October 1917 Night of Terror.
31. This ride was likely through Rock Creek Park, then as now a popular retreat from the city.
32. Professor of English and rhetoric at University of Chicago. Elizabeth likely had a graduate class with him.
33. The District government ordered closure of public gathering places due to the devastating flu epidemic.
34. Sharp and pointed, NWP's rhetoric impressed supporters but appalled those already concerned with women entering "dirty" politics.

35. Elizabeth lived in the Houston area from about age nine until she graduated from college.

36. Wadsworth's wife, Alice Hay Wadsworth, was president of the National Association Opposed to Women Suffrage.

37. "When Air Baths Should Be Taken: On awakening in the morning and several times during the day, if circumstances permit, expose your nude body to the invigorating influence of the open air and the sunlight....Where Air Baths Should Be Taken: If at all possible, air baths should be taken out of doors. Every house should have facilities for air and sun baths, that is, an enclosure where the nude body can be exposed to the open air and the sunlight." Henry Lindlahr, MD, *Nature Cure* (Chicago: Nature Cure Publishing, 1913), 327.

38. Harvey accumulated a fortune in the late 1800s and used it to purchase magazines and to fight labor union power. He was a strong suffrage supporter. He went from booster to opponent in Wilson's first campaign. The *War Weekly* contained vehement opposition to Wilson's administration and, later, to the League of Nations.

39. Winter organizing in Wyoming was not easy. As Pollitzer reported: "Snow miles high and every woman demanding a separate visit. Influenza epidemic so bad that it was considered immoral for six women to meet in a parlor....Such fearful snow, could get no billboard men to put up my big paper signs outside of the cities....I met a woman delivering newspapers, explained our campaign and my difficulties, and she offered us her eighteen-year-old daughter and a box of stickers, and we tramped the automobile roads and papered the tree trunks.... South where I have always lived (Charleston, South Carolina) so utterly unlike— When I went out to mail my thousands of circular letters each night at two a.m. funny Filipino bell boys and other kinds would escort me and carry the thousands of circular letters to mail box." See Irwin, *Woman's Party*, 329–30.

40. *Buffalo Courier*, October 22, 1918.

41. Her mother made this notation on the copy she shared with other people: "This was following her attack of influenza while she was still weak and had promised to keep out of the picketing at the Capitol steps where she and others had been rough-handled a few days previous."

42. Elizabeth shows a curious naivete and privilege. Yes, she was being abused for no reason. But the belief that "even hardened criminals" would not be treated that way? Twisting wrists is mild compared to what has been done to some perceived as criminals—in particular, suspects of a different race/ethnicity/ gender identity. And the early twentieth century was worse than the still-problematic twenty-first century.

43. Elizabeth Bass supported federal suffrage through NAWSA and disapproved of the extreme tactics of the NWP. She was director of the Women's Bureau of the Democratic National Committee, a Wilson supporter and a promoter of women's political participation. At age seventy-two, she was appointed by

President F.D. Roosevelt as supervisor of the Chicago office of the Federal Bureau of Narcotics—a "G-Man."

44. Minnehaha "Minnie" E. Brooke was an active NWP suffragist and a businesswoman. She ran multiple tearooms before opening the Brooke Farm Tea House and Inn in Chevy Chase, Maryland. She also operated a souvenir shop in downtown D.C. and became a prolific publisher of postcards. See Evelyn Gerson, "Tribute to Minnie E. Brooke," Chevy Chase Historial Soeciety, 2006, https://www.chevychasehistory.org/chevychase/tribute-minnie-e-brooke.

45. Excerpt from Stevens, *Jailed for Freedom*, 298. Germany's provisional postwar government established universal suffrage. The first elections were held in January 1919, and women won 9 percent of the seats.

46. Julia's father was a state senator from Baltimore, Maryland, who died in 1916. Julia was first heavily involved in women workers' rights, then suffrage with the NWP. She was jailed repeatedly in 1917 and 1918.

47. Merged with George Washington University in 1954.

48. Not the first. Attorney and suffragist Belva Lockwood graduated from National in 1873. She and five other women were allowed to complete a course of law, but not with the male students. Lockwood petitioned for and received her diploma.

49. Vivian Pierce later founded a nonprofit working to end capital punishment. The "part East-Indian" identification is not found elsewhere. Her grandparents were from the East Coast. Parsees are descendants of Persian immigrants to medieval India. Elizabeth's recollection of an old man and a rhinoceros is from then-popular Rudyard Kipling's *Just So Stories: How the Rhinoceros Got His Skin*.

50. Again showing naivete or willful blindness about treatment of women and men who oppose society norms. Examples at the time included union activists violently beaten or killed by police, political dissidents in peaceful rallies, etc. And she seems to ignore the treatment of non-Whites, including African American and Native American people. All these had been reported by the media.

51. Stevens, *Jailed for Freedom*, 301–4.

52. Irwin, *Woman's Party*, 465.

53. *Evening Star* (Washington, D.C.), January 6, 1919.

54. Dr. Louis K. Zinkhan, superintendent of the Washington asylum and jail. According to newspaper reports, he was fired in 1919. He had allowed a staff member to escort a prisoner, indicted for first-degree murder, to a party. The jail had also experienced several prisoner escapes. *Alexandria Gazette*, April 24, 1919.

55. The Board of Charities of the District of Columbia later gave their version of the ambulance removal: "Miss Kalb alleged that she was weak and unable to walk on account of lack of food, and in order to avoid any ground for complaint she was sent up to the city in an ambulance." Letter in Handy/Marshall Collection.

56. Probably Lucy Branham's mother, a suffragist with the same name who also did NWP work.

Chapter 3

57. *Washington Post*, February 2, 1919.
58. *Austin American Statesman*, November 26, 1919.
59. *Washington Herald*, October 18, 1919.

Chapter 4

60. With Willem van de Vall, harpist/choral director of Albion's Washington Community Opera. Letter in Handy/Marshall Collection.
61. *Washington Post*, November 7, 1920.
62. Paul, like many of the NWP leadership, supported world disarmament—just not for the NWP's work. After describing a world where women had equal rights, Paul noted that the state also must be responsible for educating all children until they came of age. And how to fund that education? "When the women of the world have junked the battleships and other impedimenta of war, enough money will be released to take care of these reforms." *Washington Herald*, October 25, 1920.
63. *Honolulu Advertiser*, March 8, 1931.
64. *Washington Times*, August 24, 1920.
65. *Washington Times*, October 15, 1920.
66. *Washington Post*, September 6, 1920.
67. *Evening Star*, October 27, 1920. In the photo of NWP women looking at ballots, note that political parties also included the Prohibition Party, the Socialists and the Farm Labor Party.
68. *Evening Star*, February 17, 1921.

Chapter 5

69. "Just Like the Men!," *New York Tribune*, March 1, 1913, Library of Congress.
70. One great leader and activist, Ida B. Wells-Barnett of Chicago, ignored the order to walk in the back with other Black Americans and simply joined the Illinois delegation anyway.
71. From the NWP Collection, Manuscript Division, Library of Congress.
72. Excerpt from Irwin, *Woman's Party*, 293.
73. Ibid., 96.
74. Editorial, *The Nation*, December 20, 1919. In the same issue, the magazine called for states to hold special sessions for ratification of the Suffrage Amendment and to do the "right thing."
75. Letter from Mary White Ovington to Harriot Stanton Blatch, December 3, 1920, National Woman's Party Papers, 1913–1974, Library of Congress; letter from Emma Wold to Harriot Stanton Blatch, Washington, D.C., December 29,

1920, National Association for the Advancement of Colored People Papers, Library of Congress.

76. *Evening Star*, February 1, 1921.

77. Daniels was an activist in New England for years. She lost land and inheritance by refusing to pay "taxes without representation." In 1917, she joined the picket line and was jailed at least three times over several years. She applauded the memory of star suffragist Inez Milholland's anti-racism efforts. Letter, National Woman's Party papers, Library of Congress.

78. See Mary Church Terrell Diary, February 10–14, 1921, Oberlin College Archives and Alison M. Parker, "Mary Church Terrell: Black Suffragist and Civil Rights Activist," National Park Service, originally published July 15, 2020, https://www.nps.gov/articles/000/mary-church-terrell-black-suffragist-and-civil-rights-activist.htm.

Chapter 6

79. In Anderson County, Texas, 1910. An estimated eighteen to two hundred Black residents were shot down in homes, fields and roads in the rural area. A special prosecutor was appointed but removed before the case could go to trial.

80. Police were often investigators, checking eligibility and making home assessments. This gave them extraordinary power in the lives of poor people. Minorities, especially, felt the pressure of this adversarial relationship.

81. Letters from the Handy/Marshall Collection.

Chapter 7

82. Mary Church Terrell, "The Mission of Meddlers," *Voice of the Negro, An Illustrated Monthly Magazine* 2 (1905).

83. For example, no picture of Terrell at an NWP event has yet been found.

84. Anna J. Cooper, *A Voice from the South. By a Black Woman of the South* (Xenia, OH: Aldine Printing House 1892), 121–22. See also Charles Lemert, ed., *The Voice of Anna Julia Cooper* (Lanham, MD: Rowman & Littlefield, 1998).

85. While the petition failed and the Trail of Tears proceeded, the effort showed some women's willingness to speak up for justice. Johanna Neuman, *And Yet They Persisted* (Hoboken, NJ: Wiley-Blackwell, 2019), 25–27.

86. "Marie Louise Bottineau Baldwin," Belmont-Paul Women's Equality National Monument, U.S. National Park Service, https://www.nps.gov/people/marie-louise-bottineau-baldwin.htm.

87. Marie Bottineau Baldwin, "Indian Women the First Suffragists and Used Recall, Chippewa Avers," *Washington Times*, August 3, 1914.

88. *Washington Herald*, February 16, 1918, Library of Congress.

89. See Katie Portante and Donald Glassman, "Kang Tung Pih, Class of 1909," August 13, 2008, *Barnard Archives and Special Collections* (blog), https://barnardarchives.wordpress.com/2008/08/13/kang-tung-pih-class-of-1909/.

90. Under Mexican and Spanish law, women could own property and defend themselves in court. This was denied to women in the United States, who on marriage gave up rights to property. See "Representation with a Hyphen: Latinas in the Fight for Women's Suffrage," National Women's History Museum and NBCUniversal Telemundo Enterprises' "Unstoppable Women" Initiative, 2020.

91. See American Foundation for the Blind, "Women's Suffrage Centennial Celebration 2020: Exploring the Activism of Helen Keller," interview with archivist Helen Selsdon.

92. See Oregon Secretary of State, "Marie Equi, M.D. (1872–1952)," https://sos.oregon.gov/archives/exhibits/suffrage/Pages/bio/equi.aspx and Michael Helquist, *Marie Equi: Radical Politics and Outlaw Passions* (Corvallis, OR: Oregon State University Press, 2015).

93. See Tara T. Green, *Love, Activism and the Respectable Life of Alice Dunbar-Nelson* (New York: Bloomsbury Academic, 2022), and Joanna Scutts, "Feminize Your Canon: Alice Dunbar-Nelson," *Paris Review*, September 28, 2020, https://www.theparisreview.org/blog/2020/09/28/feminize-your-canon-alice-dunbar-nelson/.

94. See Judy Tzu-Chun Wu, *Doctor Mom Chung of the Fair-Haired Bastards: The Life of a Wartime Celebrity* (Berkeley: University of California Press, 2005) and Malea Walker, "Dr. Margaret Chung: First American Born Chinese Woman Physician," *Library of Congress Blogs*, May 31, 2022, https://blogs.loc.gov/headlinesandheroes/2022/05/dr-margaret-chung/.

95. See Bureau of the Census, *Religious Bodies: 1906*, Bulletin 103, 2nd ed (Washington, D.C.: Government Printing Office, 1910), https://www2.census.gov/library/publications/decennial/1900/bulletins/demographic/103-religious-bodies.pdf.

96. See Kelly Marino, "We 'Protest the Unjust Treatment of Pickets': Brooklyn Suffragist Lucy Burns, Militancy in the National Woman's Party, and Prison Reform, 1917–1920," *Long Island History Journal*, June 18, 1920, https://lihj.cc.stonybrook.edu/2020/articles/we-protest-the-unjust-treatment-of-pickets-brooklyn-suffragist-lucy-burns-militancy-in-the-national-womans-party-and-prison-reform-1917-1920/, and J. Hansan, "Lucy Burns (1879–1966): Suffragette and Militant Activist on Behalf of Women's Rights," *Social Welfare History Project*, 2011, https://socialwelfare.library.vcu.edu/people/burns-lucy.

97. Selina Solomons, *How We Won the Vote* (New Woman Publishing Company, 1912), 60–65, available from the Internet Archive.

INDEX

ABOUT THE AUTHOR

Shirley Marshall is a management consultant and independent researcher. An Air Force veteran, Shirley earned a JD from the UVA School of Law. She worked in nonprofit leadership for many years, while also collecting social history ephemera. Her collection of eighteenth- to twentieth-century century correspondence proves both the complexity and the repetitiveness of history.

Inheriting Elizabeth Kalb Handy's papers led to a decades-long odyssey, exploring her full and complex life. Elizabeth's writings include her time in Washington, D.C.; in California's Sonoran Desert; and in Peking (Beijing) during the Chinese Civil War.

Other than writing, Shirley advises nonprofit clients, travels at every opportunity and tends her almost-native overgrown garden. She lives with her family in Alexandria, Virginia.

Companion website:
www.elizabethsbook.com

Includes additional material, resources and related stories.

Visit us at
www.historypress.com
....